W9-CEE-969

910703

DON MILLS

NORTH YORK
PUBLIC
LIBRARY

PLEASE KEEP CARDS IN THIS POCKET

Documents in Canadian History

LOWER CANADA IN THE 1830s

General Editor
Virginia R. Robeson

Project Team
Patrick Douglas, A. F. Flow, Alex Hewlitt,
Robert M. Laxer, Stan Pearl, Virginia R. Robeson,
Eric R. Skeoch, Peter D. Stille, and K. C. Tancock

Curriculum Series/25
The Ontario Institute for Studies in Education

THE ONTARIO INSTITUTE FOR STUDIES IN EDUCATION has three prime functions:
to conduct programs of graduate study in education, to undertake research
in education, and to assist in the implementation of the findings of educational
studies. The Institute is a college chartered by an Act of the Ontario Legislature
in 1965. It is affiliated with the University of Toronto for graduate studies purposes.
  The publications program of The Ontario Institute for Studies in
Education has been established to make available information and materials
arising from studies in education, to foster the spirit of critical inquiry,
and to provide a forum for the exchange of ideas about education.
The opinions expressed should be viewed as those of the contributors.

Cover: North shore of the St. Lawrence River, six miles east of Montreal, 1839–41,
by W. H. Bartlett.

ISBN 0-7744-0149-4   Printed in Canada

1   2   3   4   5   6   BP   28   18   08   97   87   77

Contents

IV RELIGION, EDUCATION, AND SOCIETY / 45

V POLITICS / 75

Part A: The Constitution in Theory and Practice / 78

Part B: The Politics of Confrontation / 85

Preface

Incorporated in 1970 as an independent, nonprofit organization, the Canada Studies Foundation is an experiment in voluntary interprovincial cooperation that is unique in the history of Canadian education. One of the objectives of the CSF is to identify and develop new ways of improving the quality of Canada studies in the schools so that Canadians from different regional, linguistic and cultural groups may better understand one another. To achieve this objective, the CSF encourages people from different levels of education and from different regional and linguistic groups to develop Canadian materials cooperatively.

One of the first projects sponsored by the CSF was the setting up of the Montreal/Toronto Research Group. The members of this group were French-Canadian and English-Canadian teachers of history in secondary schools in Montreal and Toronto. They worked together for five years, visiting one another's classrooms, discussing issues and topics in Canadian history and preparing resource material to be used in the teaching of Canadian history.

The material prepared by the group is unique in several ways:

— It has been developed by French Canadians and English Canadians working together.

— It has been developed by a team of teachers in consultation with academic advisors.

— It has been tested in schools in Quebec and Ontario.

— It draws together primary source material on issues and topics in Canadian history: *New France: 1713-1760, Upper Canada in the 1830s, Lower Canada in the 1830s* and *Debates about Canada's Future: 1868-1896.*

— It is accompanied by a guide for teachers providing additional information, reading lists and suggestions for using the books in the classroom.

Materials included in the books are drawn from many sources — letters, reports, diaries, speeches, books, debates, newspapers and journals. The readings were selected in order to give students experience in working with primary sources by providing a wide range of materials dealing with social, economic and political issues from different periods in Canadian history. Wherever opinions appear in the readings, efforts were made to include other readings offering opposing points of view. Conclusions are left to the reader.

It should be noted that the purpose of the books is not to examine in depth all of the issues of any one period. The members of the project team intend to provide not merely an additional source of facts for students to memorize, but, rather, an understanding of the issues and a feeling for the personalities of a particular time. Experience in the classroom has shown that great flexibility exists for using the materials, either on their own or as supplementary material to other existing sources, both primary and secondary.

Acknowledgment is gratefully given to the following institutions, without whose co-operation and financial assistance the work of the Montreal/Toronto Research Group would not have been possible:

The Scarborough Board of Education

The Toronto Board of Education

La Commission des Ecoles catholiques de Montréal

La Commission scolaire régionale Honoré-Mercier

Le Département des sciences de l'éducation de l'Université du Québec à Montréal

The greatest debt, however, is owed to the Ontario Institute for Studies in Education for its financial support and the Canada Studies Foundation for its invaluable encouragement and financial support. A very special word of thanks is extended to the directors of the Foundation from 1970 to 1975, Mr. A. B. Hodgetts, Mr. R. P. Bowles of the University of Toronto and Dr. G. S. Tomkins of the University of British Columbia. Their interest in the work of the Montreal/Toronto Research Group and their willingness to assist the group in whatever way required were greatly appreciated.

V.R.R.

Introduction

With conflicts involving English Canadians and French Canadians continually on the front pages of our newspapers, whether it be over matters of provincial autonomy, bilingualism, or separatism, the conflicts which occurred in Lower Canada in the 1830s assume an increasing significance. Like Canadians today, the people of the 1830s also faced important fundamental questions about the direction of their society. They debated these questions at times with a careful regard for the facts, at other times with much abuse of both their opponents and the truth — but almost always with passion. Yet seldom do Canadians obtain either a thorough understanding of this complicated society or a sense of the spirit of the people — their hopes, their fears, their frustrations, and their tensions, tensions so strong that they resulted in violent insurrections in 1837 and 1838. All too often, the rebellions in Lower Canada are seen simply in terms of French versus English or as a struggle between liberty-loving North Americans and reactionary Europeans. Such views, however, oversimplify a much more complex event.

Although it is difficult not to focus on the rebellions of 1837 and 1838 and see events in the 1830s as leading up to the rebellions, the documents in *Lower Canada in the 1830s* attempt to present a picture of Lower Canadian society by exploring issues and questions as seen through the eyes of people living at the time. These readings are drawn from a variety of contemporary sources: newspapers; statistics; public speeches; school textbooks; government reports, debates, and legislation; and letters, books, and journals written by settlers and visitors in Lower Canada.

Section 1, Population and Migration, discusses the nature, extent, and origin of immigration to British North America, the attitudes of the British government towards emigration from Britain to the Canadas, the opportunities immigrants expected to find in the colonies, the costs involved in emigrating, the different attitudes of Lower Canadians toward immigration, and the problems posed by emigration from Lower Canada to the United States.

The readings in Section II, Land Granting and Agriculture, deal with the land-granting policy of the colony, the different types and location of land holdings, and the problems centred around land granting and agriculture.

Economic development in British North America was not limited during the 1830s to settling and working the land. Many Lower Canadians lived in urban areas, mainly in Montreal and Quebec City, and were involved in activities associated with commerce, industry, manufacturing, transportation, and banking. Section III, Commerce, Industry, and Transportation, explores the nature of the economy of Lower Canada, indicating the relative importance of farming, trade and commerce, manufacturing, and lumbering; the economic problems and frustrations facing Lower Canadians in the 1830s; and the role

1

played by French-speaking and English-speaking Lower Canadians in the economy.

It is a relatively simple matter to develop a factual picture of Lower Canada through statistics, charts, maps, and so on. It is considerably more difficult, however, to develop a real understanding of a society, especially a society which includes people who speak two languages and who possess different cultures and values. One way to develop an understanding of a society is to examine its institutions — its schools, churches, and government — and its pastimes. The readings in Section IV, Religion, Education, and Society, cover a wide range of topics and present numerous points of view. These include the role of religion in colonial society, in everyday life, and in politics; the development of social groupings and classes; the problems posed by crime and violence; and the question of the establishment of a system of education.

The politics of the 1830s in Lower Canada seem to have been dominated by confrontation and crisis. In some areas matters seemed to be deadlocked for much of the decade. Section V, Politics, allows those living through the several crises, confrontations, and, eventually, rebellions to present them as they saw them, to express their ideas, their plans, and their frustrations. The readings outline the structure of government within which the events and discussions occurred, the attacks on and defence of the status quo, the proposals for reform, and the responses of those in a position to deal with the situation or grant reform. The readings also deal with the role played by forces such as race, religion, and nationalism in the years before the rebellions of 1837 and 1838. Events were particularly complicated in Lower Canada in the 1830s. For this reason, a detailed chronology covering the years 1791 to 1839 has been included in the book as an appendix.

I Population and Migration

The outpouring of Europeans to the New World, often called the Great Migration, gathered momentum in the second decade of the nineteenth century after the Napoleonic Wars. Lower Canada received large numbers of immigrants, primarily from the British Isles — English, Irish, Scottish, and Welsh.

The documents which are included in this section attempt to explore the major issues which were raised by this vast migration. Some of these issues focus on problems arising from the influx of large numbers of people over a short period of time; others focus on problems resulting from the fact that most of the newcomers were English-speaking, while the majority of Lower Canadians were French-speaking. Some of the issues discussed are:

1. Why did people emigrate to North America?
2. What were the motives and policies of the British government regarding immigration?
3. What were the opportunities and the problems confronting the new arrivals?
4. How were the new settlers received by the resident populations in Lower Canada? Were there differences in the attitudes of French-speaking Lower Canadians and English-speaking Lower Canadians towards immigration to Lower Canada?
5. What was the relationship between the social problems caused by immigration and the feelings of alienation and hostility which led to the rebellions of 1837 and 1838?

The section opens with a map of Lower Canada illustrating the major towns and villages and a chart indicating the growth in population from 1825 to 1844. "British Emigration Policy, 1826-30," examines the role and attitude of the British government toward immigration and the amount of assistance settlers were likely to receive when they arrived in the colony. The number of people leaving Britain for British North America and the United States is shown in Document 4.

An excerpt from a school reader used in English-language schools in Lower Canada presents a breakdown of some of the census data for 1831. The costs involved in emigrating to British North America are detailed in Document 6.

The arrival of large numbers of immigrants, mainly from Britain, was not always regarded positively by the resident population of Lower Canada (Document 7). Periodic outbreaks of cholera (Document 8), which took many lives, often coloured peoples' attitudes toward immigration. Editorials from a leading French-Canadian newspaper of the 1830s, *Le Canadien* (Document 9) present the different and changing attitudes toward immigration. The system of immigration in a colony is compared to that in an independent nation like the United States.

At the same time as the residents of Lower Canada were expressing their concern about the influx of immigrants, they were also concerned about the question of French-Canadian emigration from Lower Canada to the United States. An editorial from *La Minerve* (Document 10) raises serious questions about the justice of the British colonial system.

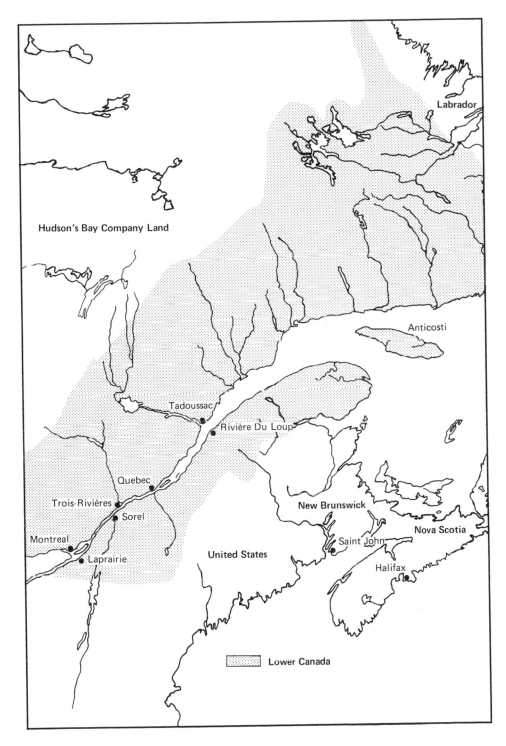

Labrador

Hudson's Bay Company Land

Anticosti

Tadoussac

Rivière Du Loup

Quebec

Trois-Rivières

Sorel

New Brunswick

Montreal

Nova Scotia

Laprairie

United States

Saint John

Halifax

Lower Canada

POPULATION OF LOWER CANADA, 1825, 1831, AND 1844

Regions	Electoral Districts	1825	1831	1844
Gaspé	Gaspé	2,108	5,003	7,146
	Bonaventure	4,317	8,809	8,246
Quebec	Saguenay	7,703	8,885	13,475
	Montmorency	7,539	8,092	8,434
	Quebec	28,683	36,173	45,676
	Portneuf	10,636	12,656	15,922
	Rimouski	7,400	10,061	17,630
	Kamouraska	12,612	14,557	17,465
	L'Islet	10,125	13,513	17,013
	Bellechasse	12,920	13,529	14,549
	Lotbinière	6,048	9,191	13,697
	Dorchester	19,052	23,846	34,817
	Megantic	204	2,288	6,449
Trois-Rivières	Champlain	5,891	6,991	10,404
	St. Maurice	13,679	16,909	20,833
	Drummond	1,825	3,566	9,374
	Yamaska	8,355	9,496	11,956
	Nicolet	11,776	12,504	16,310
St. François	Sherbrooke	4,703	7,104	13,485
	Stanstead	7,088	10,306	11,964
Montreal	Berthier	15,935	20,225	26,859
	Leinster	19,757	22,228	25,533
	Terrebonne	15,597	16,623	20,646
	Deux-Montagnes	16,700	20,905	26,835
	Outaouais	1,496	4,786	12,434
	Montreal	37,085	43,773	64,306
	Vaudreuil	11,144	13,111	17,063
	Beauharnois	14,851	16,859	28,746
	Huntingdon	28,286	29,906	36,204
	Chambly	15,000	15,483	17,155
	Vercheres	11,573	12,319	13,167
	Richelieu	15,896	16,149	20,888
	St. Hyacinthe	11,781	15,366	21,937
	Rouville	13,928	18,115	22,898
	Shefford	2,294	5,087	10,105
	Missiscoui	6,951	9,801	10,865
TOTAL		420,938	514,215	690,486

Census of Canada, 1851-1852 (Quebec, 1853), p. XVIII; and *La Minerve*, 22 March 1832.

BRITISH EMIGRATION POLICY, 1826-1830   3

Joseph Bouchette was born in Quebec City in 1774. He was trained as a surveyor and became Surveyor-General of Lower Canada in 1804. His son Robert Bouchette (1805-1879) assisted him in the preparation of his important topographical work, The British Dominions in North America *(London, 1832). Robert Bouchette took up arms in the Rebellion of 1837, was captured, and was one of those prisoners banished to Bermuda by Lord Durham in 1838. He returned to Canada from the United States in 1849 when amnesty was granted.*

In 1826 the subject [emigration] was solemnly brought before the British parliament by R. J. Wilmot Horton, Esquire, and a select committee of the house of commons was appointed "to inquire into the expediency of encouraging emigration from the United Kingdom," &c. . . .

In their first Report the committee begin by establishing three general positions: Firstly, The redundancy of the population, that is, the excess of the demand beyond the supply of labour in certain districts of England, Scotland, and Ireland, and the distressing effects of this redundancy. Secondly, The capabilities of the British colonies to subsist and provide for this surplus population; and lastly, The beneficial tendency of emigration upon the colonies themselves, and upon the national wealth, considering the colonies "as integral parts of the nation at large." Upon these grounds the expediency of emigration is recommended; but the committee, in perfect accordance with those free principles for which the institutions of Great Britain are so justly renowned, repel the idea of coercive emigration, and advise none that is not *"essentially voluntary."*

These Reports naturally apply much more to that branch of the subject which involves the consideration of the effects such a removal of the surplus population of the United Kingdom would have at home, than the investigation of its tendency, as relates to the colonies; and we are therefore precluded, consistently with our plan, from entering more fully into their contents, except insomuch as may serve to elucidate the various means proposed of providing funds, and the amount of those funds, necessary to defray the expenses attendant upon a pauper emigration.

The committee, in their third and final Report in 1827, recommend a pecuniary advance, in the nature of a loan, for the purpose of facilitating emigration, grounding their recommendation upon the success of the experiments made in 1823 and 1825, by which the ability of the emigrant eventually to refund, with interest, the monies advanced him, is abundantly established. . . .

Whether emigration should be fostered and encouraged by funds drawn from the British treasury, or be left to take its own course, is a question that has not escaped the notice of the Select Committee of the House of Commons, whose enlightened reports we have so often adverted to; and it is the opinion of the committee, that the latter principle is entirely sound, and that with some modifications, it might be beneficially acted upon; "but they conceive that it is utterly erroneous to suppose that a redundant population of absolute paupers can be removed by casual and unassisted emigration." In giving their farther consideration to this branch of the subject, the committee go on to give as their decided opinion, "that if the principle of casual and independent emigration were to be preferred to that of a regulated and located emigration, — if it were to be laid down as a principle that there could be no limitation to the absorption of labourers either in the

Market Place, Quebec City, 1840, by W. H. Bartlett

United States or in our own colonies, and that we have only to build a bridge as it were over the Atlantic to carry over the starving poor of the mother country to secure their advantage and prosperity, it will be found that the evils which would be thereby inflicted upon our pauper population would be hardly less than those from which they had escaped. If an attempt were made to pour them indiscriminately into the United States, without reference to the demand for labour that may exist there, the laws of that country, already hostile to such an introduction, would probably be made still more effectual to prevent it; or if it be proposed that our colonies should receive them in unlimited numbers when transmitted without selection, without reference to the real demand for their services as labourers, and unaided by capital, upon the principle of repayment, there will be no bounds to the complaints which the colonies will raise against the injustice and short-sightedness of our policy.

In these views of the policy of a well-regulated emigration we most fully concur, experience having already abundantly proved the distress and mischief consequent upon the absence of a regular system. The deluded pauper may gather a trifling pittance to transfer him to the colonies, and may by such a removal relieve the mother country of the burden of maintaining him and his family; but arriving in a state of absolute destitution, he finds his condition still worse in the colonies than at home, no laws existing there for the relief of the poor, indeed no such laws having been thought of in the country, from the absence of such a degree of pauperism as rendered them necessary.

It may be said, that in a country where the supply of cultivable land is exhaustless, as is the case in the British North American colonies, pauperism cannot long exist if the lands themselves be distributed to the needy upon easy conditions, and that therefore the accession of population, whether composed of indigent or wealthy individuals, provided it consist of able-bodied men, is such an accession as must be desirable in a country where the soil is so abundant and the inhabitants comparatively few. The truth of this position must be readily admitted, but the benefits to arise, from such an emigration, would essentially depend upon the facilities with which the new comers might obtain the soil which was to convert them from paupers into farmers; and if, for the sake of argument, it be assumed that the colonies had the direct control and administration of their lands, we have no doubt that the policy would be to let no man be idle whilst a farm remained to be cultivated; and thus, whilst on the one hand it would be for the interest of Great Britain to relieve herself of an unproductive labouring population, as regards their situation at home, it would, on the other, be no less an advantage to the colonies to receive it, having the means of providing for them immediately, even at the expense of an outlay of provincial capital, for which adequate returns might afterwards be received.

Joseph Bouchette, *The British Dominions in North America; or a Topographical and Statistical Description of the Provinces of Lower and Upper Canada, New Brunswick, Nova Scotia, the Islands of New Foundland, Prince Edward, and Cape Breton* (London: Longman, 1832), Vol. 2, pp. 214–219.

EMIGRATION FROM THE BRITISH ISLES TO BRITISH NORTH AMERICA AND THE UNITED STATES, 1829-1840

4

Year	British North American Colonies	United States
1829	13,307	15,678
1830	30,574	24,887
1831	58,067	23,418
1832	66,339	32,872
1833	28,808	29,109
1834	40,060	33,074
1835	15,573	26,720
1836	34,226	37,774
1837	29,884	36,770
1838	4,577	14,332
1839	12,658	33,536
1840	32,293	40,642

Parliamentary Papers, 1847, XXXIII (809), p. 39; 1861, XXII (2842), Appendix 1; 1867, XIX (3855).

5 POPULATION OF LOWER CANADA, 1835

The following excerpt is from a book published in 1835 for use in English-speaking schools in Lower Canada, probably at what we now refer to as the elementary school level. The author is described as being the "Late Preceptor of Charleston Academy, Charleston Village, Hatley." It is interesting to note that the author comments in his preface that one of the reasons for writing the book was that the only books available for use in the schools of Lower Canada were American. Other excerpts from the same school reader are found in documents 13, 17, and 45.

LESSON THIRTY-NINTH

Population

The population of Lower Canada is very small in proportion to the extent of the country. The settlements are principally confined to the banks of the large rivers, and the greatest part of the country back is still covered with forests. The whole population of the province, according to the census of 1831, was 511,917. Of these 78,729 were under five years of age, and 92,704 between the ages of five and fourteen years. Of those under fourteen, 87,774 were males, and 83,659 were females. The number of inhabited houses was 82,437, and the number of houses building was 1,458. The number of proprietors of real property was 57,891. The number of deaf and dumb persons was 408, blind 334, and insane 924. . . .

Zadock Thompson, *Geography and History of Lower Canada* (Stanstead and Sherbrooke, Lower Canada: Walton and Gaylord, 1835), pp. 12-13.

6 THE COST OF SETTLING IN BRITISH NORTH AMERICA

Another topic discussed by Joseph Bouchette in his two volumes on British North America deals with the cost to the immigrant of settling in the British colonies in North America.

Average Estimate of the Expenses of settling a Family, consisting of one Man, one Woman, and three Children, in the British North American Provinces

- Expenses of conveyance from the port of disembarkation to the place of location £10 0 0
- Provisions, viz. rations for 15 months for 1 man, 1 woman and 3 children, at 1 lb. of flour and 1 lb. of pork for each adult, and half that quantity for each child making 3^1/$_2$ rations per diem, pork being 41.5s per barrel 40 6 10
- Freight of provisions to place of settlement 1 10 10
- House for each family 2 0 0

Implements, etc.

4 Blankets	0	14	0				
1 Kettle	0	5	10				
1 Frying-pan	0	1	3				
3 Hoes	0	4	6				
1 Spade	0	2	9				
1 Wedge	0	1	4				
1 Auger	0	2	2				
1 Pick-axe	0	2	0				
2 Axes	1	0	0				
Proportion of grindstone, whipsaw and crosscut saw	0	14	0				
Freight and charges on ditto, 15 per cent	0	10	2				
Sterling	3	18	0	4	6	8	
(Equal to currency)							
Cow				4	10	0	
Medicines and medical attendance				1	0	0	
Seed corn	0	1	6				
Potatoes, 5 bushels at 2s.6d	0	12	6				
				0	14	0	
Proportion of the expenses of building for the depot[1]				1	0	0	
Ditto for clerks, issuers and surveyors to show the lots[1]				1	5	0	
£60. sterling is equal to				66	13	4	

Joseph Bouchette, *The British Dominions in North America; or a Topographical and Statistical Description of the Provinces of Lower and Upper Canada, New Brunswick, Nova Scotia, the Islands of New Foundland, Prince Edward, and Cape Breton* (London: Longman, 1832), Vol. 1, p. 286.

Note
1. Newcomers were required to pay fees to officials performing certain services for them.

INDIGENT IMMIGRANTS, 1830   7

This editorial appeared in La Minerve *on 30 August 1830. One of the leading political newspapers in Lower Canada,* La Minerve *was founded in Montreal in 1826 by Auguste-Norbert Morin and Ludger Duvernay, and supported the radical French-Canadian views of Louis-Joseph Papineau and his followers. Duvernay and Morin fled to the United States after the Rebellion of 1837, but Duvernay returned to Canada in 1842 and resumed the editorship of* La Minerve. *The paper ceased publication in 1899.*

Up until now we have paid no particular attention to the plan debated in the United Kingdom to send some of the millions of poor to the colony. In England alone, the poor received six or seven million pounds from the wealthier classes according to law. This amount does not include the enormous sums raised by almsgiving and charitable contributions. The egotism and inhumanity of this plan were so obvious. It was so unjust to the colonies, so impractical as a means of permanent relief for the mother country and bound to be so disastrous for the colonies as well as for the poor themselves, that we thought they would never think seriously of implementing it. We have, nevertheless . . . indisputable proof that the trouble has already begun. In both the city and the country, we have seen paupers sent here by the state authorities begging for alms. Despite the customary charity of the people of the land, who voluntarily support their own poor and who have been able to give them some aid, this cannot last. It is totally beyond the resources of the colony to support a large number of lamentable victims of life, the luxury, the misfortune and the excessive taxation of the mother country. It is unrealistic to suppose that people whose spirit of independence has been crushed and who, by relying on public support, have lost the habit and ability to keep their needs within the limits of their resources, will be able to make their living in the colonies where in reality a man needs more to keep himself and his family alive than in the mother country. If the system continues to any great extent, these unfortunate people are destined to perish miserably from disease and suffering, and to bring the colonies to the same degree of poverty.

As long as emigration was restricted to people who emigrated on their own funds, we could be sure up to a point that the emigrants were industrious and careful people, and they were welcome; but the moment emigration is effected by means of subscription or state authority, we no longer have any assurance as to the ability of the emigrant to support himself. He is an indigent who is perhaps used to depending on others for his living and his presence is dangerous and is a burden to both the emigrant who has already arrived and to the older residents. In many of the States, laws have been passed imposing severe penalties for bringing in emigrants like this. We can expect these laws to be adopted everywhere and, as a result, to have our own difficulty increased. In the colonies our only means of protection is to protest to the imperial government which could, at least, put a stop to this evil by prohibiting the authorities from intervening in emigration to the colonies with resources other than those of the emigrants themselves.

We do not think it possible that the British government would countenance the enormous project of sending the poor from a rich country where they can be supported to another country which is comparatively poor where they would surely perish.

---

8   CHOLERA IN THE QUEBEC CITY AREA: G. J. MOUNTAIN, 1832

George Jehoshaphat Mountain, son of Jacob Mountain, the first Anglican bishop of Quebec, was born in 1789. He became his father's secretary in 1811 and was made rector of Quebec and archdeacon of Lower Canada in 1821. Consecrated Bishop of Montreal in 1836, he became Bishop of Quebec in 1837, remaining in that post until his death in 1863.

According to the census taken in pursuance of the Provincial Act of 1831, the population of the City and Banlieue of Quebec amounted then, in round numbers, to something more than 28,000, of whom nearly 21,000 were Roman Catholics, very nearly 5,000 of the Church of England, and the remainder (approaching towards 2,500) of other Protestant denominations. As far as has been hitherto ascertained, the whole number of deaths by Cholera in the following year (1832) has amounted to 2,800. From these data it would appear that the whole population has been decimated by the pestilence; but besides some increase of the resident population, on the one hand, it has to be taken into the account, on the other, that the *transient* population of the summer, (whatever proportion it may have borne to the whole), furnished many subjects for the melancholy list — the disease having prevailed among such of the Emigrants as landed and among the sailors also in port.

The number of interments by the Ministers of the Church of England, during the whole of the year 1831, was 382. In 1832, it was not far short of that number in the month of June alone, and in the whole year has amounted to 975. The total of interments from Cholera among the whole Protestant population is estimated at 785. Upon the two consecutive days, however, mentioned in the Sermon, (the 15th and 16th of June), upon each of which upwards of 70 were interred by myself, it appears probable that among the bodies sent from the hospital to the Church of England burial-ground in the distracting confusion which then prevailed, there was a considerable proportion of Roman Catholics and very possibly were some Protestants of other communions. . . .

Never can the scene be forgotten by those who witnessed it, which was exhibited in the dusk of one evening, at the Emigrant Hospital, before the forced exertions of some members and agents of the Board of Health had provided another building in the Lower Town exclusively for the reception of cholera patients. A house opposite to the hospital had been engaged to afford additional accommodation, but the unfortunate subjects for admission came pouring in before any arrangements at all sufficient could be completed, and the desertion, in one afternoon, of part of the servants who had been hired, rendered the attendance, before most inadequate, so miserably inefficient, that the passages and floors were strewed with dying persons, writhing under wants to which it was impossible to minister, some of whom, I believe, actually died before they could be got to a bed. The Health Commissioners, the head of the Medical Staff, and the first Medical practitioners of the city were upon the spot together, and doing all they could, but how could their skill or judgement meet all the exigencies of such a moment? Women were met at the doors bewailing their affliction, who had come too late to take a last look at their husband while alive: parents or children were surrounding the death-beds of those dear to them: patients were, some clamoring in vain for assistance, some moaning in the extremity of languor, some shrieking or shouting under the sharp action of cramps; friends of the sufferers were contending angrily with the bewildered assistants. . . .

The Clergy in passing through some quarters of the town to visit the sick, were assailed sometimes by importunate competitors for their services, — persons rushing out of the doors or calling to them from windows to implore their attendance upon their respective friends, and each insisting upon the more imperative urgency of the case for which he pleaded. . . .

The conveyance of bodies to the burial-grounds in open carts piled up with coffins continued after the Board of Health had provided covered vehicles for this purpose (attached to the hospitals, but disposable for the same purpose elsewhere), from the unavoidable insufficiency of the provision. I saw upon one occasion twelve bodies thus conveyed from *one* hospital and at *one* time to the *Roman Catholic* place of interment *alone*. Many fables were abroad among the lower orders, respecting persons said to have been buried alive in consequence of the order for their interment within a certain number of hours. . . .

The symptoms, in general, were much less horrible, although the disease, I believe, was equally fatal, among children. I do not remember to have seen an instance in which they were affected by the cramps. I saw two little things of the same family, lying, one day, in the same bed, at the hospital, to die quietly together like babes in the wood. . . .

It was one of the characteristic circumstances of the time, that boards were put up in various quarters of the town with the inscription *COFFINS MADE HERE*. . . .

Appendix, *A Retrospect of the Summer and Autumn of 1832; being a Sermon delivered in the Cathedral Church of Quebec on Sunday, the 30th of December, in that Year*. By the Venerable G. J. Mountain, D. D. Archdeacon of Quebec, Rector of the Parish of Quebec and Examining Chaplain to the Lord Bishop of Quebec (Quebec: Thomas Cary & Co., 1833), pp. 21-25.

---

9   CRITICISM OF IMMIGRATION POLICY:
LE CANADIEN, 1832-1833

The French-language newspaper Le Canadien, *from which the following extracts are taken, was founded in Quebec City in 1806 to act as a defender of French-Canadian institutions, laws, and language.* Le Canadien *was frequently suppressed for its anti-government views. When these editorials appeared in 1833 it was edited by Etienne Parent, who achieved an outstanding reputation as a journalist.*

Le Canadien, October 12, 1832

. . . *Canadiens*[1] will never look unfavourably on the honest and industrious immigrant who arrives among them and who comes to help them work towards the development of this new and vast country, without thought of infringing upon and dominating the people. But, if *Canadiens* see that England's parishes are banding together in order to rid themselves of their poor and burden a young country like theirs with the dregs of England, Ireland and Scotland; if they see rich and powerful companies assisted by the government and in connection with the party which in that colony has long dreamed of domination and the destruction of every thing Canadian; if they see that this policy of annihilation is being preached openly in the meetings of these Companies; if, based on the behaviour of the immigrants from the different parts of the three realms in state affairs, they see this iniquitous plan being carried out — would they not have had to renounce all feeling of honour and nationality if they did not look with some suspicion on this multitude of foreigners who flock in every year under these circumstances? Can one blame them for seeing in these floods of immigrants instruments of tyranny and oppression which the old enemies of our laws and institutions will make use in proper time and place? Add to that also, seeing every possible facility offered to these foreigners while *Canadiens* are exposed to every imaginable difficulty without having a system which is right for them.

Le Canadien, April 1, 1833.

. . . We do not think it sound policy, either for England or for this colony, considering the special circumstances in which the country finds itself, to fill this province with emigrants from Great Britain. However, under a totally local system of government, the country would be interested in attracting industry and men from overseas. Emigrants would, therefore, no longer enter this country with prejudices and ideas of control and domination which conflict with the feelings and interests of the *Canadien* people and which will create terrible difficulties for the next generation. A government ruling in the interests of the people would rid the political order of this group of schemers and creatures who take advantage of their factitious power to foment division and thus succeed in dominating. The two people, having one single and common purpose, would not take long to join forces and would work in harmony for the progress of the country. The newcomers would feel that it was just and more reasonable that a few thousand men arriving year by year conform to the customs of the country than that one-half a million men adopt their customs. If it is in the laws of Providence that this country should one day lose some of its distinctive traits, let this be left to the action of time, to the force of circumstances. These two forces always operate without friction and without danger. But it is dangerous for man to touch these inflammable materials; the least shock produces a spark, and the spark an explosion.

Le Canadien, May 15, 1833.

The different articles we have published on the endeavours of the country's enemies have brought us up to present time. The audacity of oligarchy has only increased with time and its attitude is more menacing than ever. Having established a base for its destructive operations through the act of tenure, it has left no stone unturned in its search for ways of gaining its ends safely and promptly. It was not enough to banish *Canadiens* from the uncultivated lands of the country; they had to erect a higher barrier, and they found one in the transplantation of a foreign population. Thus, they summoned emigration by every possible means. For the benefit of the oppressed people of the United Kingdom, they painted a picture of Canada as a sort of promised land. All one had to do to get rich quickly was to set foot on the land — the poor and oppressed of the United Kingdom flocked to our shores. Those who came with some resources and a disposition for work have succeeded in acquiring the affluence which any hardworking man can achieve in America. The others perished from misery. . . . This charming picture of the country they painted was destined to have the greatest effect on the most wretched people of the United Kingdom; also the bulk of emigration came from Ireland, a Catholic country which is also the most oppressed in the civilized world. On their arrival, the Irish were not long in seeing that they were working towards the very system which had forced them to leave their homeland and joined the cause of the people they had been sent to crush. One of the party leaders said in a meeting in London about a year ago that they would have to stop sending Irishmen to Canada because they were too much in sympathy with *Canadiens*. We have had occasion to discuss this sinister plot with respect to its pernicious effects on the general well-being of the country. Today we consider it to be only one of the plans the oligarchy has set to work in order to get rid of the *Canadien* people.

Le Canadien, August 2, 1833.

We have come to the fourth chapter of Mr. Lebrun's[2] work, which deals with emigration. His European readers must have had reason to be surprised when he informed them that in Lower Canada, which contains millions of acres of uncultivated land, emigration is regarded unfavourably. But what people would not be afraid, when gangs of emigrants openly announce that they are sent to this country to subjugate us? This statement would have gone unnoticed, if it were not linked to a thousand other circumstances which serve to prove that there exists a long-standing, systematic plan to erase, to wipe out, if possible, the *Canadien* people and their institutions. Emigration has been seized upon as one of the many ways of accomplishing this aim. It is of little wonder that we mistrust emigration based on such a principle. We must consider it in much the same way as the Roman provinces once considered the invasions of Goths and Vandals, except that they at least left ruins and fragments behind their swath of destruction so the people could rebuild their social structure. However, if our enemies had their way, the descendants of those courageous colonists who established civilization on the banks of the St. Lawrence, amidst extraordinary trials and tribulations, would be forever overshadowed on Canadian soil. Thus the arrogant policy of a party which receives too much attention and is too influential in the assemblies, turns what is seen as beneficial elsewhere, into an evil for this country. Our neighbours to the south invite European proletarians from every nation to come and reduce the huge western forests to cultivated land. Furthermore, the emigrant does not go there, nor is he summoned there, to destroy the laws, customs and institutions of his adoptive land; he arrives with the intention of conforming to the institutions, customs and laws he will find established. Let it not be said that because the United States has an independent, sovereign government, then what is good, just and proper for these states is not so for Lower Canada because it is a dependant province; since, as far as justice is concerned, we derive from treaties and actual laws, the rights which our neighbours derive from their political position. . . .

Notes
1. The term *Canadiens* in this reading refers to French Canadians.
2. Writer and teacher, who wrote about Canada in the 1820s. See Document 28.

10 FRENCH-CANADIAN MIGRATION TO THE UNITED STATES, 1836

La Minerve, May 26, 1836.

The Montreal *Gazette*[1] announces that a large number of Canadians are leaving the banks of the Richelieu and environs to go and settle in Michigan and other parts of the United States. According to this newspaper, more than 500 people with this aim have apparently embarked at St. Jean.

Most of them are young men who are going to look for more liberal institutions elsewhere. It appears that they are not the only ones who wish to go and try their luck abroad. Every day, the steamboats take away a certain number of people who are taking this course. It seems to me that nothing is better suited to showing us the corruption of our institutions. Not only does foreign emigration barely touch our shores, but the natives themselves are starting to emigrate, from a country which has barely 500,000 people, and where more than half of the land is still uncultivated! Difficulties arising from all quarters in the concession of these lands, the limited exit of Canadian goods which results from our exclusive system of trade with England, poor administration, these are the real causes of this sizeable emigration. The newspapers of Upper Canada inform us that approximately the same situation prevails in that province. These facts alone say more against the present colonial system than would several volumes.

Notes
1. Montreal *Gazette*. The oldest (1778) continuously issued newspaper in Canada and the first newspaper published in Montreal. It was published in French and English at first, but began publishing in English only in 1822. This was in part a reflection of the rapid growth of the English population.

II *Land Granting and Agriculture*

Agriculture and the policy of land distribution helped to determine the distribution of the population in the Canadas. The population in Lower Canada had been well established for more than two hundred years, while the population in Upper Canada was relatively new in the 1830s. Land companies were mainly responsible for the distribution of land. This situation gave rise to several abuses. Speculation became common. In Lower Canada, the habitant living on seigneurial land differed from the settler in the townships in both Upper and Lower Canada. In fact, French Canadians found it difficult to accept the British settlers moving into the Eastern Townships of Lower Canada, which had a new system of land granting.

The readings in this section deal with issues raised by the following questions:

1. What was the relationship between agriculture and settlement in Lower Canada?
2. How was land distributed?
3. What were the weaknesses of the land-granting system as seen by people living at the time?
4. What was the importance of the land companies? How effective were they in settling land in Lower Canada?
5. What place did French Canadians have in agriculture?

The first document in this section illustrates the layout of a seigneury. The following document by Laterrière (Document 12) describes the relationship between the seigneur and the *censitaire*. Not all land in Lower Canada was held according to the seigneurial system. The British government, in part to attract British settlers to Lower Canada, allowed land to be divided and held according to the township system used in Upper Canada. Document 13 provides useful background information about the townships and seigneuries of Lower Canada. Next, the official policy of granting land in Lower Canada is discussed by a commission to W. B. Felton on granting land. Document 15, an excerpt from *Le Canadien*, deals with some of the problems and abuses in the land-granting system, such as land speculation. Edmund O'Callaghan, an opponent of the land-granting system, presents evidence in Document 16 against the British American Land Company.

Document 17, an excerpt from a geography and history reader used in Lower Canada in the 1830s, presents information of the soil and crops found in the province. The last three documents, "Economic Difficulties in Lower Canada, 1833," "The Backwardness of Lower Canada in Agriculture, 1836" and "Quebec Agricultural Report, 1836," discuss both the technical and human difficulties relating to agriculture in Lower Canada.

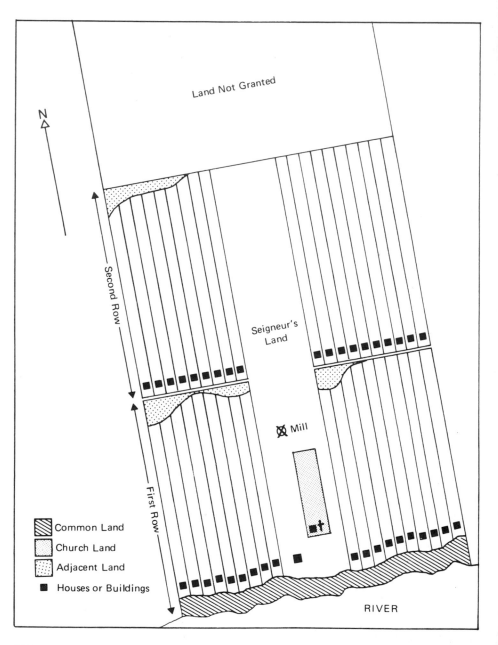

Note

The dimensions of an average seigneury were about 24 to 48 kilometres in depth by 6½ kilometres in width. Land conceded to the habitants generally measured 3 arpents by 30 arpents. An arpent was a linear measure used in Canada and was approximately 60 metres in length. As a measure of area, an arpent was equal to about .34 hectares.

SEIGNEURIAL TENURE OF LAND IN LOWER CANADA, 1830

12

Pierre de Sales Laterrière was born in Quebec in 1785. He studied medicine in Quebec City and in London, England. He later decided to return to Lower Canada, and took over his father's practice in Quebec City. He was known to be sympathetic to the views of the reformers. In 1830, under the pseudonym of "A Canadian," he published A Political and Historical Account of Lower Canada, with remarks on the present situation of the people, as regards their manners, character, religion, etc. *from which the following is taken.*

By the laws of the country, the *tenure* of the land is of that sort termed *en fief* or *seigneurie*; that is, a lord, or *seigneur*, possesses a right to certain returns over a specific portion of territory, each portion, thus possessed, being termed a *seigneurie*. The returns consist, partly in personal service, partly in certain taxes upon production and interchange at the hands of the vassal; on the other side, the lord, or *seigneur*, is bound to perform certain acts for the convenience of his vassal: he must build mills, make roads, etc. The returns, on the part of the vassal, are usually moderate; and thus, at present, no very great distinction exists between the class of *seigneurs*, and that of vassals. Still, however, this is a distinction, destined in process of time to become more marked and important. Already there is a partial political influence exercised by the *seigneurs* —exercised it yet has indeed been entirely for the interests of the whole people: the time may come when they will prove a landed aristocracy, exercising an overbearing and pernicious influence over the fortunes of their countrymen. In the present stage of society, nevertheless, all the highest degree of intelligence possessed by the people is to be found either among this class, or those sprung from the mercantile community, who, in fact, from their wealth, have been enabled, by purchase, to form the chief part of the seigneurs of the country. This division of the people into seigneurs, and *not* seigneurs, is, as far as regards future consequences, by far the most important division now existing among them. That division, however, which at present is most marked, is that of the people of the towns, and the people of the country; which last have a distinctive name, and are now universally termed, *par excellence*, LES HABITANTS. The manners of these two classes, though in the main and essential particulars greatly similar, still exhibit many and striking differences. The people of the towns, from their constant communications with the English and Americans, have lost many of the peculiarities still retained by the more simple people of the country: wealth has introduced into the cities European refinements and luxuries which, to our forefathers, were completely unknown; to that, if we are desirous of obtaining a true picture of *Canadian* manners and customs we must penetrate into the country, and mingle with the artless and unsophisticated inhabitants still to be found there.

Pierre de Sales Laterrière, *A Political and Historical Account of Lower Canada, with remarks on the present situation of the people. as regards their manners, character, religion, etc.* (London: Marsh and Miller, 1830), pp. 118-119.

Steamboat wharf, Montreal, 1832, by J. Duncan. The "Queen" was a market steamer, bringing farmers with their produce from nearby parishes.

13   SEIGNEURIES AND TOWNSHIPS, 1835

The following excerpt is taken from a book written by a teacher for use in English-speaking schools in Lower Canada.

LESSON FIFTH

Seigniories and Townships

Lower Canada is not all divided into Townships. This country was first settled by the French and they divided the land upon which they settled into *Seigniories* and *Fiefs*. The seigniories are not all the same size. Some of them are much bigger than a township, and some are much smaller. The fiefs are generally much smaller than townships. All the country along the rivers St. Lawrence and Richelieu on both sides, is laid out into Seigniories. The inhabitants of the Seigniories are nearly all of French origin. The townships are situated back from the large rivers, and along the Ottawa, and settled by people from England, Scotland, Ireland, and the United States. The people of French origin and who speak the French language, amount to about four fifths of the whole population of Lower Canada. The remaining one fifth are of the other origins above named, and speak the English language. The seigniories were granted while Canada was under the government of France. The townships have all been granted since Canada has belonged to Great Britain. The greatest part of the townships are situated in the southeastern part of the province between Vermont and the river St. Lawrence, and are known by the name *Eastern Townships*.[1] The Eastern Townships are mostly embraced by the following counties, namely; Megantic, Sherbrooke, Stanstead, Drummond, Shefford and Missisco.

Zadock Thompson, *Geography and History of Lower Canada* (Stanstead and Sherbrooke, Lower Canada: Walton and Gaylord, 1835), pp. 12-13.

Note
1. The region was given the name Eastern Townships to distinguish if from the townships west of Montreal, in what is now Ontario. Until 1791 the area included in the Eastern Townships was largely an unbroken wilderness. In 1791 the law of free and common socage was passed in Lower Canada, which led to the surveying and granting of land free of the conditions laid down for land purchase under the seigneurial system. The first settlers in the Eastern Townships were of British stock, chiefly United Empire Loyalists from New England. The Eastern Townships were officially established by an act of the legislature of Lower Canada in 1829.

LAND POLICY IN LOWER CANADA, 1826   14

Instructions to a land commissioner concerning the sale of waste lands in Lower Canada.

WASTE LANDS OF THE CROWN
Commission to W. B. Felton

. . . That no Lands or other Crown Reserve arising from Lands within the Province of Lower Canada be hereafter disposed of or Granted except upon the following Conditions.

By actual Sale or in Cases of Poor Settlers, by Grants subject to Quit Rents in the manner hereafter directed.

That you do from time to time, and at least once in every Year submit to the Governor or Officer Administering the Government a Report of the Total quantity of [sic] each District of Crown Property within each District of the Reserve so far as you may then have ascertained the same together with your opinion of the quality of each description of Property which it may be expedient to offer for sale within the then ensuing Year and the upset Price per Acre at which you would recommend the several descriptions of Property to be offered obtaining previously a Certificate from the Surveyor General of Woods and Forests within the Province that the Land proposed to be offered to you does not contain any considerable quantity of Valuable Timber fit for His Majesty's Navy or for any other purposes, it being the intention that no Grant of the Land upon which such Timber, may be growing should be made until the Timber is cleared.

That no lot should contain more than 1200 Estimated Acres.

That no Land be granted at any other time than at the Current Sales in each District except upon application from Poor Settlers who may not have been in the Colony more than 6 Months preceeding the last annual Sale; That Settlers so circumstanced may be permitted to purchase Land not exceeding two hundred Acres each at the price at which it may have been offered at the last annual Sale, and not purchased and may pay for the same or by Quit Rent computed at 5 p^r Cent on the Sale Price and thenceforth these Persons shall be considered as entitled to all the privileges, and be subject to the same obligations as they would have been subject to, if they had purchased the Land at the last Sale. . . .

Documents Relating to the Constitutional History of Canada, 1819–1828. Selected and edited with notes by Arthur G. Doughty and Norah Story (Ottawa, 1935), p. 349.

---

15   LAND SPECULATION IN LOWER CANADA, 1833

Le Canadien, July 19, 1833.

Freed of monopolies after the conquest [by the British], the colony made rapid progress, and in 70 years a population of 60 odd thousand grew to half a million without any external addition. Unfortunately news of the past few days makes one fear for the future of the country, much the same as in the past. Once again Canada is threatened by the terrible regime of Companies of foreign speculators. There is no longer any doubt that the land company of Lower Canada will go into operation soon and its first attempt will be to take possession of 300,000 to 500,000 acres of land which it will dispose of as it sees fit; but to the best possible advantage, since the goal of this company like the former companies of New France will not be to settle the country but to make money. The intention and the wish of the Assembly was to give away the land free or almost free to those willing to undertake the difficult task of clearing the land, and it was for that purpose that it granted huge sums of money to open roads in the Townships. This money came from the wallets of each one of us; it increased the value of the uncultivated land; was it not right that the people, the poor settler who was born here or elsewhere should be the sole beneficiary of this increase in value? For quite a while the government has not ceased shouting about Interior Communication, about facilities to offer the new settlers who could not penetrate the forests without roads; it has shouted so much and so loudly, and its shouts seemed so sensible and to have so useful a goal, that for several years in succession our representatives have thrown the treasury contents in every direction, and were it not for low finances and fear of a national debt, only God knows where they would have stopped. Their liberality, however, has been such that expensive roads now cross the uncultivated land of the country.

---

16   OBJECTIONS TO THE BRITISH NORTH AMERICAN LAND COMPANY: EDMUND O'CALLAGHAN, 1833

Edmund O'Callaghan — doctor, politican, journalist, and historian — was born in Ireland in 1797 and came to Canada in 1823. He was the editor of the English-language

Montreal newspaper the Vindicator *from 1834 to 1837. Elected to the Lower Canadian Assembly in 1834 as a radical and a supporter of Papineau, he took part in the Rebellion of 1837 and fled to the United States, following the wrecking of the offices of the* Vindicator, *when a warrant was issued for his arrest. He never returned to Canada.*

The North American Land Company, which is the subject of this editorial in the Vindicator *on 21 May 1833, was organized in England in 1832. The company acquired large tracts of land in the Eastern Townships of Lower Canada for the purpose of settling English immigrants.*

. . . Objection 1st. — The establishment of a Land or any other chartered Trading Company within the province, not only without the consent and authority, but against the will of the local legislature, is, to say the least, impolitic in the Home Government, inasmuch as it is an insult to the legislature of the country, and an infraction of the Constitution of 1791, by granting which the Imperial Parliament vitually gave up all right to meddle in the regulation of our internal affairs.

2d. — The Land Company deriving its existence from authority out of the province, is not, as it ought to be, responsible to the Provincial Legislature, which is the highest authority in the country.

3d. — The funds to be derived from the Company, in return for the lands which they may purchase, not being under the control, nor at the disposal of the responsible branch of the Legislature, it is to be presumed that they will be expended in a similar manner to those derived from the sale of lands to the Upper Canada Company — i.e. partly in rendering an irresponsibile executive independent of the people; partly in pensioning place holders, legislative councillors, churchmen and others; and partly in endowing colleges of an exclusive religious character; and all this without the consent of the House of Assembly, on whose authority alone public monies can be constitutionally expended.

4th. — Experience teaches us that a country never prospers whose trade and resources are in the hands of a company. Monopoly is a curse which cramps the energies of a people and whilst it bloats itself, impoverishes the land. . . . If corporate bodies and monopolies are such a blessing, what, we ask, prevents the clergy reserves from being settled? They are in the hands of a corporation. They are monopolyzed. Yet they scarcely bring £50 per annum. — And, again there are the Crown Reserves which together with those belonging to the Church form 2/7ths of the whole of the waste lands of the province, and are besides the greatest nuisance the province groans under, why are not these disposed of and alienated! Because the people will not be humbugged into becoming cotters,[1] tenants and dependent on others when they can so easily become free and independent proprietors. If the prosperity of a people be one object of a government, let it leave each individual to manage his own affairs. — The country will reap the benefit. Once interfere and general confusion will inevitably ensue.

5th. — Should the Company go into operation, it is only just that it should have some profit in return for the capital it lays out. . . . [The profit to be derived, however, comes] from the sweat, labour and hard work of the poor emigrant, who will take their [the Company's] lands, but who, if he gets along unconnected with them, will have these profits in his own pocket, to be laid out in improving his farm — in educating his children, in clothing his family, providing for them in case of sickness, etc. whereas under the system which the [Montreal] *Herald*[2] prays for, these profits will be exported to London, there to be squandered in luxury and dissipation by a race of speculating *absentees*, regardless alike of the happiness, existence or rights of the people of Lower Canada. Is there, we ask, a poor industrious husbandman who would willingly or knowingly lend himself to a scheme such as this, fraught with such permanent evils to himself, his progeny and the country? a scheme whereby the rich will be made richer, and the poor, poorer.

6th. — A company the establishment of which we resist, will always be surrounded by a numerous retinue of agents, clerks, servants and dependents, who can easily be converted into spies, informers and petty tyrants, to execute the orders of their employers, whereby an unpopular or encroaching government will always have at its command, a regularly organized body of abettors to aid them in crushing or stifling public opinion at elections in case of a political struggle, and for the purpose of getting up addressees in favour of the administration, should an obnoxious governor as in times of yore, be called on to give an account of his stewardship. Moreover, the deceptive system of liberal credit on which the company will dispose of their lands, will ever prevent the settler becoming independent. In plain terms, he will always remain a slave, and should a poor man whose spirit is too independent to crouch to the proprietor or agent, refuse to vote as he is directed, woe be to him; away with his improvements to the hammer — or if not in debt, the neighbourhood will be made too hot for him, and he must sell out perhaps to his ruin, and remove. There will be no mercy for him.

7th. — This company by a preference of the class of buyers will, besides, uphold, foster and perpetuate national distinctions, which have ever been the bane of the province and which our governors unfortunately have always encouraged, forgetful that they are sent out for the good of *all* and not to lend themselves to the self-interested views of the *few*. . . . Instead of being united and happy, the people of the province will be

Davis's Clearing, Eastern Townships, Lower Canada, 1839–41, by W. H. Bartlett

divided one against another. They will be taught to believe that they have separate interests; they will be kept apart by the machinations of those who fatten on the abuses against which we have so long complained. . . . Such are the unfortunate consequences to be dreaded from the establishment of the Lower Canada Land Company which we are all called upon to resist, as we love ourselves, our prosperity and our country.

If the *Herald* has the welfare and the interest of the emigrant at heart, why does he not second the exertions the Assembly have, in vain, been making, for so many years, to get the management of the wild lands, for the purpose of giving them for *nothing* or at a very small price to those who will actually settle on and reclaim them. It is admitted by all political economists, that wild land is intrinsically of no value, and that it becomes valuable only according to the sum of labour expended on it. Therefore, we say give it to the actual settler without distinction of origin, for nothing. If it yields anything afterwards, it will be much more advantageous for the tiller of the soil to retain the profits for himself, than to have them sent to England to be spent by gentlemen jobbers, whom he shall never see, and who were he hungry, naked or otherwise in distress, would never relieve him.

Notes
1. A word used in Scotland to describe a person occupying a small holding of land, originally in return for service.
2. Montreal *Herald* (1811-1959). In the years before the Rebellion of 1837 it opposed the advocates of rebellion and employed a number of brilliant men in its campaign.

SOILS AND CROPS, 1835   17

The following excerpt is taken from a school reader published in Lower Canada in 1835 and intended for use in English-speaking elementary schools.

LESSON THIRTY-SEVENTH

Crops and Productions

There is a great difference in the soil of Lower Canada, being in some places remarkably good and in others poor. Along the great rivers the soil is generally rich and productive, and in most of that part of the country denominated the Eastern Townships, it is of superior quality. There are, however, some considerable tracts in the province, which are so rough and barren as not to admit of cultivation, particularly northern and eastern parts. Swamps are common in different sections, but they are not generally extensive. The hill lands, when cleared, afford excellent pasturage, and the low banks and many of the swamps may be burned into meadows. The lands, which admit of being ploughed, are generally a rich loam, are easily cultivated and produce plentiful crops. The different kinds of grass grow well in all the parts. The most certain and profitable crops are wheat, oats, peas, rye, barley, buck wheat and potatoes. Indian corn in some seasons does well, but on account of the shortness of the summer and early frosts, it is considered an uncertain crop. Flax and hemp grow well, and most of the various garden vegetables.

Apples, plums and cherries are produced in tolerable perfection in many parts. Currants are cultivated in almost every garden, and gooseberries thrive well when cultivated. There is also a variety of wild fruits and berries.

Zadock Thompson, *Geography and History of Lower Canada* (Stanstead and Sherbrooke, Lower Canada: Walton and Gaylord, 1835), p. 55.

---

18 ECONOMIC DIFFICULTIES IN LOWER CANADA, 1833

La Minerve, December 23, 1833.

The crop of last season was of a very mediocre quality in Lower Canada, and it was much smaller than those of previous years; it could be said that in certain parts of this province it was a total failure. This autumn the amount reaching the market was minimal, and it was sold, for the most part, to be milled. . . . In Upper Canada the crop was plentiful; several shipments of new wheat have been sent this autumn. . . . Various reasons can be established for the decline of commerce in dry goods. The total cessation of commerce in early June 1832 due to the dreadful ravages of cholera, a situation which lasted during the entire season, constitutes the beginning; since then the difficulties have been mounting. The crop below Quebec failed last year and this year. The non-payment of the civil list, of which more than £50,000 is out of circulation, is definitely having its effect, but the principal cause is an overabundant importation of goods.

---

19 THE BACKWARDNESS OF LOWER CANADA IN AGRICULTURE, 1836

La Minerve, July 1, 1836.

It has often been stressed in *La Minerve* that the farmers of this country would profit from lending some care to agricultural management, and also from varying their crops, instead of completely neglecting the first, as they do, and in the case of the second, clinging obstinately to old routines, constantly following a system which may have been good once, but which no longer suits present circumstances. It is no doubt proper to stick almost exclusively to the cultivation of wheat on newly cleared lands which are covered with a thick layer of humus formed by the decomposition of trees and other plant-life, built up over the centuries, and where vegetation, hardly in need of the stimulus of fertilizers, often has too much vigour. But it must be understood that once this layer is exhausted, when the land needs fertilizer to stimulate a lifeless vegetation, it becomes fundamentally necessary to change the method of cultivation and to adapt it to this new state of affairs in order that it may be profitable. Ultimately, one must have recourse to imitating the cultivation methods of areas settled long ago.

We will not enter here into detailed consideration, already exposed to the public several times, of the necessity for the farmer to devote himself to the breeding of animals in order to increase his profits, and especially the necessity to possess many cows which procure him the means of making and selling proportionate quantities of butter and cheese, besides increasing his supply of fertilizer) He should also maintain young animals and he should raise pigs in particular. It is apparent also that in order to carry this out the farmer must cultivate vegetables on a large scale, and it has been seen that a farmer can quite quickly double his production and make a good living on a piece of land which would otherwise barely support him and his family, if he pays attention to these aims. Indeed, apart from the benefits of which we have just spoken, there is then a great abundance of manure to restore the necessary fecundity to his land, to say nothing of the fact that the growing of vegetables prepares the soil for the cultivation of grain in such a way that the subsequent yield of grain is doubled.

QUEBEC AGRICULTURAL REPORT, JULY 1836   **20**

The Quebec Gazette *(1764–1924) in its early years was published twice a week in both languages. For many years it contained only a summary of the news, but this began to change around 1810. The publisher from 1793 to 1848 was John Neilson, a friend and sympathizer of the French Canadians. He was also a firm defender of the British connection and a believer in law and order. This report appeared in the* Gazette *on 1 August 1836.*

During the sixteen years that we have furnished Agricultural Reports for the Quebec *Gazette*, we never sat down to the task with such unfavourable forebodings as at present.

The drought noticed in our report for June has continued during two months; till the 29th July, nothing but some light showers occurred to allay its destructive effects on every kind of vegetation. The heat was excessive in the first week of the month; the thermometer having been, on several days, at 98° in the shade. It was succeeded by parching, clear, easterly winds, and then, alternately, cool, clear, and warm days, till the close of the month. All the rains that fell never penetrated more than an inch into the ground, which remained underneath like a dry cake. . . . The leaves on many trees became drooping and withered, and all of them began to shed their leaves. The wells, springs and streams were dried up, fires raged in the woods, and extended to the low mossy grounds. . . .

Hay-making commenced about the middle of the month, or rather, on more than one-half of the meadows the mowers cut down a dried stubble, or withered grass, not worthy of the name of hay. It is only on low, rich lands that there is anything like a crop.

Turnip-seed sown at the usual time did not come up for want of moisture, and the ground cleared and mowed for the purpose, is still bare and unproductive, although it has been sown several times in hope of rain.

The late sown potatoes did not come up or only here and there a stalk. The early sown ones, although presenting a tolerable appearance above ground, have no tubers, or if there is anything like a potatoe at the foot, it is sprouted, and the other roots running into puny stalks, instead of forming potatoes.

The oats and peas are stunted, and will be unproductive excepting on low lands. Barley is also short and of doubtful appearance.

Wheat is the best crop, and will probably be an average on all low lands. . . .

In fact, never in the memory of the oldest inhabitants have the prospects of the harvest been so unfavourable in this vicinity. It behoves the poorer classes to exert all their industry and practise the greatest economy and foresight, to provide the necessaries of life for the ensuing winter. It behoves the wealthier classes to remember that they are the "stewards of the poor," to waste nothing, and be prepared for the calls that will be made on them. . . .

III Commerce, Industry, and Transportation

The aim of the documents in this section is to illustrate certain aspects of the economy of Lower Canada during the 1830s. Included under the general headings of commerce, industry, and transportation are such topics as the banking and money system of Lower Canada, the insignificant role of French Canadians in the economy, and the organization and structure of trade between Britain and the colonies. The readings in this section deal with the following questions:

1. What was the basis of the economy of the Canadas during the 1830s?
2. To what extent did the banking system of the 1830s meet the economic needs of the Canadas?
3. What role did French Canadians and English Canadians play in trade and industry?
4. What was the nature of the transportation system in the 1830s?
5. How was trade in the Canadas integrated into the economic system of Great Britain?

The author of the first reading in this section discusses the commerce and manufacturing found in Lower Canada. In the following document, Henry Bliss presents statistics for British North America on foreign trade. An excerpt from the Montreal *Gazette* in Document 23 discusses the serious economic situation in 1834. The life of people involved in the timber trade is presented in the next two readings. Document 26 describes the poor facilities for land transportation in Lower Canada. The role of French-speaking and English-speaking businessmen in trade and industry, which was a topic of much concern in Lower Canada, is discussed in documents 27 to 30, which conclude this section.

21 COMMERCE IN LOWER CANADA, 1837

In his preface to the book from which this excerpt is taken, the author describes it as a "Humble Attempt to Spread Information Upon a Subject Deeply Affecting the Interests of the Peasantry in Particular," and dedicates it to the "Magistrates and Landlords of the Over-populous Districts of the United Kingdom." He also states that the "opinions herein are freely expressed, respecting the conditions of the American Colonies and the character and prospects of the great body of the settlers that inhabit them, are the result of nearly twenty years' personal observation."

The commerce of the colony [Lower Canada] consists in the export of timber, furs, wheat, pot and pearl-ash, and the import of almost every article manufactured in Great Britain. A thousand ships annually visit the ports of Quebec and Montreal, for the prosecution of this beneficial intercourse. The consumption of British goods in this province does not, however, bear the same proportion of the population as the consumption of our manufacturing in those colonies where the inhabitants are more exclusively English. The French descendants, except around the towns, are for the most part, alike unacquainted with the luxuries and the wants of more recent settlers, while many of the necessaries of life are produced by the extreme industry of their women. . . .

The proper manufactures of [Lower] Canada are inconsiderable, and are almost wholly for internal consumption. There are foundries and stove-manufactories established at Three Rivers, where iron . . . is found of very superior quality and in great abundance. And, at Montreal, there is a manufactory, where steam-engines are made of dimension and force to suit enormous boats which navigate the Canadian waters; but they are not equal in workmanship to those which are sent from England. There are also breweries, distilleries, and soap and candle manufactories.

S. S. Hill, *The Emigrant's Introduction to an Acquaintance with the British American Colonies, and the Present Condition and Prospects of the Colonists* (London: Parbury and Co., 1837), pp. 124–125.

22 FOREIGN TRADE: HENRY BLISS, 1830–1831

The lawyer and author Henry Bliss was born in New Brunswick in 1797. For many years he was agent for New Brunswick in Britain. In this document Henry Bliss gives figures for the total imports and exports from the ports of Quebec City; Prince Edward Island; St. John's, Newfoundland; Saint John, New Brunswick; and St. Andrew's and Halifax, Nova Scotia.

Since the year 1825, the North American colonial ports have been thrown open to all nations. Those provinces are now treated commercially as so many counties in the

United Kingdom. There is no part of the world with which they are prohibited from trading as freely as the merchants of Glasgow or Liverpool. No advantage could be more specious, more popular, more vaunted, as well by those who conferred as those who received the boon. But like many other objects of common esteem or plausible theory, it will not stand the test of statistics. Upon such examination it shrinks to that class of commercial benefits, which are much more easily adorned with seducing epithets and pompous abstractions, than verified by experiment and official returns.

It is now about twenty years since the free ports of the Northern Colonies have been partially opened, and during the last six years their intercourse with all nations has been entirely emancipated by act of parliament; yet their trade with foreign countries is of all the most unimportant, the least improving, and the least beneficial. The reason is obvious. Their best markets are found within the British dominions. There the productions of colonial industry meet protection; in foreign countries, with the exception of Portugal, they find none. Thus almost the whole colonial trade is essentially a home trade.

NUMBER OF SHIPS, TONS AND MEN EMPLOYED IN THE TRADE OF THE NORTHERN COLONIES WITH ALL FOREIGN COUNTRIES ACCORDING TO OFFICIAL RETURNS. . . .

1830

	Inwards			Outwards		
	Ships	Tons	Men	Ships	Tons	Men
Total British	1,362	71,917	5,028	509	42,513	2,677
Total Foreign	438	52,819	2,142	431	54,633	2,190
Total of both	1,800	124,736	7,170	940	97,146	4,867

1831

	Inwards			Outwards		
	Ships	Tons	Men	Ships	Tons	Men
Total British	1,127	68,690	4,524	646	55,912	3,275
Total Foreign	221	16,506	989	146	15,292	845
Total of both	1,348	85,196	5,513	792	71,204	4,120

. . . As the American trade is perhaps the greater in amount of navigation employed, though not in value of the articles exchanged, statistics of the intercourse with that country follow next. . . .

NUMBER OF SHIPS, TONS, AND MEN EMPLOYED IN THE TRADE OF THE NORTHERN COLONIES WITH THE UNITED STATES ACCORDING TO OFFICIAL RETURNS. . . .

1830

	Inwards			Outwards		
	Ships	Tons	Men	Ships	Tons	Men
Total British Vessels	280	22,809	1,191	254	10,455	706
Total Foreign	421	52,804	2,225	431	54,633	2,002
Total	701	75,613	3,416	685	65,088	2,708

	Inwards			Outwards		
	Ships	Tons	Men	Ships	Tons	Men
Total British Vessels	574	41,367	2,243	416	27,182	1,527
Total Foreign	162	16,567	895	150	15,724	864
Total	736	57,934	3,138	566	42,906	2,391

It is sufficiently evident from this, that the maritime commerce between those Colonies and the United States, is of no great importance for the value of articles exchanged. . . .

The trade with other foreign countries is of far greater value to colonial industry, and considering the length of the voyage usually made, is more important to British navigation, than the maritime intercourse with the United States. The articles exported are all of native production, fish, victual and timber; and the proceeds are in general remitted to the United Kingdom, and contribute to discharge the balance due for British manufacturers. . . .

This trade with foreign Europe and South America admits of being yearly and permanently extended in all those productions which are brought down the broad St. Lawrence, and also, it is to be hoped, by the inexhaustible fisheries of the Gulph, the coasts and rivers of British America. Of these exports it may be presumed that far the greater part will ever be carried under the British flag. . . .

Henry Bliss, *The Colonial System; Statistics of the Trade, Industry and Resources of Canada and the other Plantations in British America* (London: John Richardson, 1833), pp. 111-121.

23 THE STATE OF THE ECONOMY, 1834

Originally published in both French and English, the Montreal Gazette *was published in English only from 1822. This was, in part, a reflection of the rapid growth of the English population in Montreal. This editorial is taken from the issue of 6 September 1834.*

COMMERCIAL REMARKS ON THE MONTREAL MARKET

Since our last report there has been a moderate return of activity to our Trade. The usual stagnation of the season has given way, and auction sales are now going on to a considerable extent. The dreadful scourge[1] with which we have been visited, but which happily has now entirely subsided, does not appear to have produced the same disastrous effects upon our trade, as in 1832. It broke out when the spring trade was over, and has ceased before the fall trade can be said to have commenced. From the peculiar state of the money market in New York in 1833, the stagnation was even more decided than during the present season. In one of our weekly reviews last year, namely, that for the 23d. July, we said "with the exception of West India produce every thing is dull, in fact there is nothing doing in sales, every one complains of the scarcity of money, the Banks not even discounting to retire paper.'' At the same period the state of affairs was certainly worse in 1834. On the 6th August, 1833 we wrote "the business transactions during the week have been but limited, smaller indeed than in the previous week.'' On the 14th August we characterized business transactions as "unusually small for the season.'' The week ending 21st August, was "fully as dull as the preceding," and it was not until the 3d. of September that we were enabled to say, "the business done in the past week, though moderate, has far exceeded that of any other during the last six weeks, and may be considered as indicating the commencement of the fall trade.'' We have said enough to show that the commencement of the fall trade of 1834 has not been retarded, and we think also, to prove, that the cholera has not exercised any serious influence upon the trade.

It appears to us that our prospects are by no means disheartening. Providence hath blessed the labours of our husbandmen with a most abundant return, a circumstance which must ever act favourably upon trade; and the state of the American Money market is such as to produce confidence and credit, and, we think, to preserve it, and our own importations are sufficiently moderate to promote an improved state of our market. We think, therefore, we are fully justified in offering these cheering reflections to our commercial readers.

Note
1. The word "scourge" is used in this document to refer to the outbreak of cholera.

LUMBERING IN THE CANADAS: JOHN MACTAGGART, 1829   24

John Mactaggart was a British engineer and geologist who worked for the government as Clerk of the Works on the Rideau Canal from 1826 to 1828. During this time he had the opportunity to observe the life of the lumbermen in the Canadas.

Lumbermen are persons who procure logs of timber, deals, planks, spars, staves, &c. in the forest, and bring them down the wild lakes and rivers to market. The term "lumber" is quite applicable; for what are these wooden wares but lumber? In winter they *make it* on the remote banks of small streams; and when these swell with the spring freshets, it is floated into the larger, of which they are branches, where there is never any scarcity of water, and where they can have no dread of being detained for the season. Often the thaw is such, that the small rivers do not rise; the consequence is, that the lumber must remain, in hopes that the next spring will be more favourable. This is a misfortune, however, to those in the trade; at least, with those who have it in such a situation. Those who can get it to market, however, obtain a better price for the commodity. The tributary streams of the Ottawa, or Grand River, such as the Madawaska, Bonchère, and Calumie, are those where the *Lumberman's* operations are, at present, the most extensive in Canada. They will average about 700 miles from Quebec.

Lumbermen and *Shantymen* are nearly synonymous; with this difference, that the former are generally the masters, or, what the Canadians call, the *Bourgeois* of the latter.

Mills at Sherbrooke, Lower Canada, 1839-41, by W. H. Bartlett

The *Shantymen* live in hordes of from thirty to forty together; throughout the day they cut down the pine trees, and square them in the *pineries*, or the oaks in the groves, and afterwards draw the logs to what is termed the *bank*, with oxen. When spring draws on, they form the lumber into small rafts, called *cribs*, and drop away down the rapids to market. When they come to any extensive sheets of still-water, the cribs are brought into one grand flotilla; masts, white flags, and sails are sported; while, with long rude oars, they contrive to glide slowly along. Thus they will come from Lake Alumet, on the Ottawa, to Wolfe's Cove, Quebec, a distance of nearly 800 miles, in about six weeks. On these rafts they have a fire for cooking, burning on a sandy hearth; and places to sleep in, formed of broad stripes of bark, resembling the half of a cylinder, the arch about four feet high, and in length about eight. To these *beds*, or *lairs, trams* or *handles* are attached, so that they can be moved about from *crib* to *crib*, or from crib to the shore, as circumstances render it necessary. When they are passing a *breaking-up rapid*, they live ashore in these lairs, until the raft is *new withed*, and fixed on the still-water below.

As these people live in huts in the woods, as stated, which huts are houses only for a season, they are called *shanties*, and hence, *shantymen*; but there is something more attached to the name *shanty* than mere *hut*, in the lumberman's dictionary. Thus, so many men, oxen, so much port, flour, &c. compose a *shanty*. A *beehive*, with him, is not one, unless it be stocked with bees, combs, honey, &c. In these shanties they pass the time pretty well, considering them to be made up of Highlandmen, Irishmen, and Yankees. Great quantities of spurious whisky are swallowed, many battles fought, and so forth; yet these things being perfectly natural to the shantyman, he could hardly endure life without them. In the conceited towns he is held in abhorrence by the *clerk* and *counter-jumper*, who know no more of the laws of Nature, or the elements of human life, than a parcel of magpies. They fancy that the wood-cutter from the wilderness should be made up of nods and smiles, starch and ruffles, like their dear affected selves, never thinking that he is a creature by himself, like the sailor, bred amid dangers and difficulties, and made somewhat roguish by the sharking rogues of the cities. But the *storekeepers* cram their stuffs into their shanties, almost whether the poor fellows will or no, giving long credit; and if they do not get three times the value for them, they *decoy* the lumberman, who probably had himself nearly drowned in the rapids, and his raft spread about in all directions, the chief part never to be obtained again.

The truth is, that the lumberman can do very well without the *storekeeper*, but the latter not without the former; so the man of intrusion decoys the man of real business. The lumberman, with all his roughness of manner, is the person who does good to the country. He brings an article to market with much risk — the only staple commodity, in fact, that is; and, consequently, he is the means of bringing the greater portion of cash to Canada. . . . What is a *storekeeper* but a person living on his exertions, — a person that might be dispensed with. . . .

John Mactaggart, *Three Years in Canada: An Account of the Actual State of the Country in 1826-7-8. Comprehensing its resources, productions, improvements, and capabilities; including sketches of the state of society, advice to emigrants, &c.* (London: Henry Colburn, 1829), Vol. I, pp. 320-325.

THE LIFE OF THE LUMBERERS: **25**
FRED FITZGERALD, 1826

Fred Fitzgerald (1804-1861) was a lieutenant in the British navy who served in Canada and the United States. This excerpt is taken from his narrative, published in 1827.

It is curious that in Quebec, the only memorial of Wolfe should be a little quaint wooden figure, set up in a niche at the corner of an old French house; but we should also recollect that Quebec was a conquered city, and but little interested in preserving the memory of its victor.

The precipitous path by which our troops ascended the heights, is now a road to the different coves that contain the timber brought down by the rafts. The river, in this part, is covered with fleets of timber-ships, which are in a state of constant activity.

On a strip of land, under the nearly perpendicular bank, are the wretched dwellings of the Lumberers, as the raftsmen, voyagers, and others whose business it is to supply the timber trade, are called. Their mode of life is peculiar: — They proceed in their canoes to the interior, and uncleared country, where they fell the timber, depending for subsistence upon the produce of the forests and rivers. When they have collected a sufficient quantity of wood, they form rafts, and float down by its various tributary streams into the St. Lawrence, which conveys them to Montreal and Quebec, where they sell the product of their labour.

From the moment that they receive their money, a scene of uproar and debauchery commences, which concludes only when the whole of it is gone. This state of things is the more dreadful, as, from the nature of their employment, they are semi-barbarians, and their savage jubilees often lead to the perpetration of the most atrocious crimes.

Oil wells, Gaspé, Lower Canada, 1834, by Thomas Pye

When their money is spent, they retire to the woods, re-commence their labours, and return to a repetition of the same dangerous and degrading excesses.

Fred Fitzgerald Deroos, *Personal Narrative of Travels in the United States and Canada in 1826* (London: William Harrison Ainsworth, 1827), p. 207.

26 ROADS IN LOWER CANADA: THOMAS SCOTT, 1829

Thomas Scott from Quebec City testifying before a committee of the Assembly of Lower Canada, 1829.

. . . Because of the poor state of the roads the farmers and others remote from Quebec cannot bring produce to market, with the result that in certain seasons of the year the market at Quebec is poorly stocked and people ask exorbitant prices for goods. There is no encouragement whatsoever for immigrants to go and settle on uncultivated land which could be profitably cultivated if it were possible to bring the products to a good market. The committee cannot be unaware, since it is an established fact based on the experience of all European countries, that the formation of good roads is the first step in the development of a country, and although it costs a lot at first, it is an expense which in time and even quite promptly will render the most advantageous results. In this new country which is in the process of improvement as is Lower Canada, it is particularly desirable to begin as soon as possible and to pursue this undertaking as energetically as means will allow. At certain times of the year, the main roads are hardly passable, as one can imagine by observing that in spring and autumn the mail from Montreal to Quebec frequently takes seventy hours to travel a road of about 180 miles, whereas the mail in England in any season does not take twenty-four hours to cover the same distance. As for the roads in the vicinity of Quebec, they are so bad in autumn and spring that the mail coaches take three hours to go the last eight miles and a carriage with a single horse can carry no more than 300 pounds and that at approximately two miles an hour. This results in a considerable rise in the price of furs, goods and merchandise for the consumer without which the merchant would get no equivalent profit.

Journal de l'Assemblée legislative du Bas-Canada, 1828–1829, Appendix U, 10 January 1829.

FRENCH CANADIANS AND COMMERCE: *LA MINERVE*, 1829

27

La Minerve, July 13, 1829 (a letter to the editor).
Let us speak about commerce. Perhaps it is in this area that Canadians [i.e., French Canadians] have the greatest obstacle to overcome. They have not done their best in this area. First, very few Canadians know about commerce as something they have studied and learned. Occasionally we have even found people engaged in commerce claiming that it is not worth studying. And we know that it is a fairly common error among us to think that one can know about things without having studied them. The Canadians who were formerly engaged in trade have gradually withdrawn. They did not form any establishments of significance. Even now there is hardly what one could properly call an association, a Canadian trading association. Yet without this it is almost impossible to trade extensively. It cannot be said that they have always been and still are completely without capital. It is said that they have often had reason to complain about the lack of exactitude on the part of those whom they dealt with, here and in England, in order to get merchandise from them when they wanted to attempt overseas trade. It is possible to suspect that these complaints were well-founded. But why trust others for things you can handle yourself? When, particularly in trade, have we ever found that we could count on the care, attention and the vigilance of an agent as we could count on ourselves? Anyway, trade in this country in particular requires local knowledge. Only Canadians could make a good choice of merchandise which is suitable to the inhabitants of the province. Are there many Canadians who cross the ocean themselves to supervise the purchase or choice of goods to be imported? By doing this they would save the commissions, the discounts, by which the intermediary agents who are between them and the European manufacturer or producer profit. You will say perhaps that the person who has an acquired capital runs too much risk in a country where trade is too often in a

state of fluctuation which can bring about the ruin of those engaged in speculations of this nature if they are fairly substantial. But this danger is like any other; it is up to prudence and know-how to avoid it. Another thing, why do those who have capital not unite? Why do they not form with those who deserve their confidence joint stock companies which would protect them from losing anything but a small stake? If this business were just successful on one occasion, they could congratulate themselves on having made for themselves and their Compatriots a significant and lasting source of prosperity. What an advantage it would be, moreover, for the country to have connections which would make it and its inhabitants known to others. Do you think it would be as easy to slander them as has too often happened on the other side of the ocean? Do you think that Mr. McGillivray would have dared to speak about Canadian merchants and about this country in the insulting manner he did last year before the committee of the House of Commons of England if there had been even a half-dozen respectable associations of merchants either from Canada or closely linked to Canadian trade associations?

Let us admit it honestly. We still suffer much too much from the vices of the former institutions of the past. We lack activity and union in this matter just as we have lacked it for so long, just as we still lack it at times on the subject of public affairs. Don't petty interests of localities, of parishes, of counties, of districts still paralyse at times the reunited efforts of the country's inhabitants to free ourselves from this sort of tutelage? A small number of men managed to place us and keep us under this tutelage for so long by using one group against the rest and to take over the place that belongs to all of us.

28   A FRENCH-CANADIAN BUSINESS FIRM: ISIDORE LEBRUN, 1833

Isidore Lebrun was a French literary figure and teacher who, following a visit to Canada, wrote a book on his observations in 1833.

At last business in Lower Canada is receiving a strong stimulus from patriotism. A Canadian business firm is being organized, a limited partnership, whose head office will be in Montreal, and which will have agencies or branches in Liverpool and London. On March 7, 1832, more than 100 Canadians of French origin adopted the following resolutions: "This assembly notes with deepest regret that the import and export business, handled in the past exclusively by Canadians, has passed into the hands of our co-subjects from overseas; that Canadians have not until now profited from population growth and from the rapid development of the resources of the country; that foreign commerce is closely linked with domestic commerce and with agriculture, and that they should mutually aid each other; that the need to open the extensive field of business to our youth is becoming alarmingly obvious, especially since we shall fear even to educate our children, because we shall not know where to direct them after their studies. . . ."

Isidore Lebrun, *Tableau statistique et politique des deux Canadas* (Quebec: Neilson et Cowan, 1833), pp. 413–414.

Timber depot near Quebec City, 1839-41, by W. H. Bartlett

PROGRESS OF FRENCH-CANADIAN INDUSTRY: *LA MINERVE*, 1830

29

La Minerve, December 16, 1830.

For quite some time the correspondence of *La Minerve* has dealt with the position of industry amongst us and with the necessity of working towards its development and progress. We cannot but admire the zeal of those who are busy calling the attention of their fellow citizens to public affairs. However, I do not know just how much we deserve their reproaches. Perhaps it would also be wise to consider the numerous difficulties we have had to overcome in the way of instruction, particularly the impediments the enemies of the country's well-being and development have always placed in our path. Luckily the impetus has already been given: these obstacles are disappearing more and more and the present generation, enlightened by the lamp of education, taught by the patriotism and experience of its ancestors, cannot fail to reach a high degree of civilization.

For the moment, I will limit myself to quoting a fact which cannot be too well-known. One of our fellow citizens, Mr. P. P. Lachapelle, of the Côte des Neiges, has succeeded in grinding flour which is equal in every respect to the flour we receive from the upper province or the United States. Bakers who use this flour are reputed to make the best bread. You will undoubtedly take pleasure in learning how Mr. Lachapelle was able to give this degree of superiority to this product of public consumption.

After being involved in the construction of mills for a long time and noting how much inferior in quality the flour produced there was, Mr. Lachapelle travelled to Upper

Canada and the United States. The result of his observations was that he only had to clean the wheat perfectly to get as good a flour as his neighbours. To reach his proposed goal, it was, therefore, simply a matter of following their example in the construction of the sieves and imitating them in attaching brushes. This is what he did; but in perfecting this invention, he substituted wire in the fibres which makes the operation easier and more economical. . . . This accomplishment deserves our praise.

In this matter we cannot stress too much the advantage which would result from the formation of an association for competition and public service. Made up of Canadian [i.e., French-Canadian] citizens who would work in harmony to make known the position of the arts and sciences in foreign countries, and to introduce useful discoveries or inventions, to diffuse them among our compatriots, an association like this would be above all a powerful means of spurring competition by making known those in this country who are devoting themselves to a certain branch of industry and by marking them as worthy of public attention and of the esteem of their fellow citizens.

How rapidly Canadians, who have so often proved to have happy dispositions, would progress in this sort of prosperity and take the place due to them. Let us hope that this oft-repeated appeal to the most noble of sentiments will not be without results. In the meantime, we cannot urge the residents of this land too strongly to take advantage of research and observations and to follow the example of one of their respected compatriots.

30 ECONOMIC DOMINATION BY THE ENGLISH, 1837

The Constitutional Association of the City of Montreal was a group of English-speaking Lower Canadians who opposed the ideas and reforms proposed by French-speaking Lower Canadians.

It must also be observed that the general trade of the Province is carried on almost exclusively by the Colonists of British origin. The French-Canadian inhabitants have never had much share in it, and the general indisposition evinced by them to commercial pursuits, has almost become an anti-commercial spirit. The inhabitants of British origin have always formed, and will continue to form the commercial part of society, and possessing the superiority of commercial wealth, enterprise and intelligence, must always command a superiority in this respect. Some French-Canadian institutions of a commercial character, have been lately formed, but their extent does not impugn the general principle above stated; these exceptions go to establish the correctness of the observation, which may be further confirmed by reference to the following statement of the amounts of stock in the public undertakings of the District of Montreal, held by the inhabitants of the two races [see table opposite].

This indisposition manifested to commercial pursuits, by the inhabitants of French origin, materially affects the inter-Provincial trade, injures the general trade of the Provinces with Great Britain and Ireland, and will force much of the British shipping employed in it to other shores. The evil effects are even at present being exhibited in Upper Canada, where a desire has been manifested to obtain other channels of communi-

	Capital		Shares	British	French
1. Stock of the Bank of Montreal	£250,000		5,000	£247,400	£ 2,600
2. Do. of City Bank	200,000		8,000	192,805	7,200
3. Do. of Champlain & St. Lawrence Railroad Company	50,000		1,000	49,150	850
4. Do. Montreal Water Works	70,000		80	70,000	
5. Do. of St. Lawrence Steamboat Company	65,000		48	61,615	3,385
6. Do. Montreal Steam Tow Boat Company	40,200	present value	710	38,508	1,682
7. Do. Ottawa and Rideau Forwarding Company	33,190	,,	1,172	32,482	708
8. Do. St. Lawrence Steamboat and Mail Coach Company	25,000	,,	1,000	25,000	
9. Do. Montreal Gas Works	20,000		1,000	19,500	600
10. Do. St. Ann Market	15,500	cost paid		13,575	1,925
11. Do. of other Steam Boats and capital invested in the forwarding establishments on the Saint Lawrence, above & below Montreal	50,000			50,000	
	£818,890			£819,940	£18,950

French-Canadian Institutions

	Capital		Shares	British	French
1. Stock of Mutual Insurance Company	40,000			16,281	23,719
2. Do. Banque du Peuple- People's Bank	80,000	supposed		30,000	50,000
	£938,890			£866,221	£92,669

cation than the St. Lawrence, for the supply of the necessities, and the disposal of the surplus produce of that Province; and unless prevented by an early adoption of the proposed Legislative Union, the sea-ports of the United States, and especially New York, will become the great marts of the trade of Upper Canada; indeed an application to the Government of the United States was lately made by a number of individuals engaged in commerce in that Province, praying that goods for Upper Canada might be landed at New York free of duty.

Constitutional Association of Montreal, *Representation on the Legislative Union of the Provinces of Upper and Lower Canada* (Montreal: Arnour and Ramsay, 1837), pp. 16–19.

IV *Religion, Education, and Society*

Society in Lower Canada in the 1830s was shaped in part by the conditions created by the Conquest of 1760 and the coming of the English, and in part by the forces at work in the Atlantic world of the early nineteenth century. The period after the Conquest resulted in a society of two peoples, two languages, and two cultures. The early decades of the nineteenth century quickly exposed the colonies to the harsh effects of British industrialism. As a result of British attempts to solve some of the problems of the industrial revolution, succeeding waves of British immigrants arrived in the colonies. Between 1828 and 1838 the population of Lower Canada increased substantially. The presence of these immigrants posed a serious threat to the settled community of Lower Canada. Problems resulting from the influx of large numbers of people over a short period were made even more difficult to resolve because of differences in language and culture.

The documents in this section address themselves to certain questions:

1. What kind of future faced newcomers to Lower Canada?
2. How did Lower Canada, with its French-speaking majority and its long-established society, respond to the arrival of more and more English-speaking people?
3. How could the commercial values of the English-speaking Lower Canadians coexist with the very different social values of French-speaking Lower Canadians?
4. What difficulties did people from such varied backgrounds and holding such different views on religion, politics, education, and social values face in creating a viable community?
5. How influential was religion in setting the tone of society in Lower Canada?
6. To what extent was the Roman Catholic Church involved in the political life of Lower Canada?
7. To what extent did the school system reflect the values of society?

The first two documents in this section (31 and 32) described conditions in Quebec City and Montreal in 1839. Both writers, Murray and Bosworth, present readers back in Britain, many of whom would be prospective emigrants, with factual accounts of the physical and social aspects of the two towns. These documents are followed by three excerpts from Tocqueville's description of Lower Canada and its people, all of them expressing his delight in finding a French society still surviving in North America. In Document 34, Laterrière discusses how the differences between French-speaking and English-speaking Lower Canadians affected the class structure of Lower Canada.

Girod, a Swiss, describes the social life of French Canadians in town and country and the impact of newcomers from Britain. Hugh Murray in Document 36 gives his impression of the habitants. In Document 37, Bouchette describes the characteristics of the British population of the Eastern Townships, where many of the immigrants settled. Document 38 by Isidore Lebrun gives details about crime and punishment in Lower Canada.

The next four readings deal with religion. The first document presents the number of people belonging to the major religious groups in Lower Canada in 1831. Document 40 is an editorial from *Le Canadien* in praise of the French Roman Catholic clergy. Both the excerpt from *L'Ami du peuple* in Document 41 and Bourget's letter (Document 42) defend the participation of the clergy in politics.

Etienne Parent, writing in *Le Canadien*, argues strongly for the advantages of two languages (Document 43). Documents 44 to 49 deal with education and schools. The number of schools and students in Lower Canada from 1828 to 1835 is presented in Document 44. Document 45 is a lesson from a school reader giving details about the education system in Lower Canada. Document 46, a letter in *La Minerve* from a teacher, argues for energetic steps to deal with illiteracy and ignorance. The next reading, "How to Remedy the Situation in Education," discusses practical ways to improve schools and teachers. The document on the *fabriques* (vestry boards) reveals some of the problems of financing schools and shows the close relationship between the church and education at the parish level. Newton Bosworth (Document 49) compares attitudes toward schooling held by French-speaking and English-speaking Lower Canadians.

31

This description was written by Hugh Murray in his book An Historical and Descriptive Account of British America. *The author had never visited North America, and drew his information from his own wide reading, and from other people with experience of the colonies, including Sir George Simpson, Governor of the Hudson's Bay Company.*

In the midst of this fine landscape stands Quebec, the capital of British America. It is seated on a promontory stretching out into the river, which, by means of it and Point Levi on the opposite side, is narrowed to about three quarters of a mile, though immediately below it spreads out into a wide basin. . . .

The scenery of Quebec and the surrounding country is described by all travellers as rivalling in picturesque beauty the most favoured parts of the earth. The navigator who ascends the St. Lawrence, after he has passed the Isle of Orleans and entered the broad basin already mentioned, where he first comes in sight of this capital, is struck with intense admiration. He sees its citadel crowning a lofty cliff, its castle and batteries overhanging a range of formidable steeps, the river crowded with numerous vessels of every form and size, from the hugh timber-raft to the bark canoe. . . .

Quebec, from its situation and the care with which it has been fortified, is a very strong town, and considered the chief bulwark of British America. On the summit of the lofty headland just described, stands the citadel. . . .

The upper town, which these fortifications enclose, forms the chief part of Quebec, and the residence of all the principal inhabitants not engaged in trade. It is a tolerably handsome old-looking town; the houses being mostly of stone, partly roofed with tin. . . .

Of religious edifices the chief is the Roman Catholic cathedral, being 216 feet long by 180 in breadth, and capable of containing a congregation of 4,000. The interior has a lofty and solemn aspect, but the outside is heavy and not in very good taste. There are several other Catholic churches. The English cathedral, though smaller, being only 136 feet long by 75 broad, and in a simple style, is considered extremely neat. The Scotch church is much inferior. The monastic establishments are spacious. The Hotel-Dieu, founded in 1637 by the Duchess d'Aiguillion, includes a convent, church and courtyard, besides cemetery and gardens. The range of buildings is extensive, but without any ornament; and its chief use is as an hospital, in which respect it affords the greatest benefit to the colony. A prioress and thirty-two nuns are continually employed in ministering to the sick, with a great degree of attention and skill: hence government have been induced to make occasional grants in addition to the considerable revenues attached to the establishment. The Ursuline convent is a neat building in the heart of the city, surrounded by fine gardens. It was founded in 1639 by Madame de la Peltrie, chiefly for the purposes of education. The inmates, forty-six in number, observe a somewhat rigid seclusion, but they instruct, in reading, writing, and needlework, a certain number of girls, comprehending even Protestants. They are very assiduous in embroidery and other ornamental works, especially for ecclesiastical vestments; and the fruits of their industry are often sold at high prices, which are thrown into the common stock. The spacious monastery of the Jesuits, 224 feet by 200, surrounded by noble gardens, was forfeited on the suppression of that order, and at the conquest was regarded as crown property. It was then converted into a place of exercise for the troops, and to the regret of many its fine tress were cut down; but the legislature of the province have lately petitioned for its being restored to its original purpose of education. The large edifice called the Seminary, with an extensive domain attached to it, was founded in 1663 by M. de Petre, with a view to the instruction of the Catholic clergy. It is now open to all students of that persuasion, who are initiated in the different branches of knowledge upon paying the trifling sum of 5s. annually to defray incidental expenses. Pupils, indeed, may be boarded as well as taught for £12, 10s. year. . . .

The lower town is a narrow crowded range of buildings, extending along the base of the precipice. The spot on which it stands is entirely the creation of human industry; for originally the waves at high water beat the very foot of the rock. Wharfs, however, have been founded and carried out into the river, though nowhere further than 240 yards; and on these streets have been erected. So limited, indeed, is the space that the quarter beyond Cape Diamond communicates with the rest only by a path cut in many places through the solid rock. This part of Quebec is compared to the most irregular and confused districts of Edinburgh. It is connected with the upper town by what is called Mountain Street, which formerly was not passable for carriages without extreme difficulty, but has of late been much improved. The Breakneck Stairs, as they are denominated, are more commodious for foot passengers. Besides extensive wharfs, the lower town contains the Quebec Bank, which, in addition to apartments for its appropriate purpose, has others for a fire assurance company and a subscription library, the most extensive and valuable in Canada. . . .

Quebec maintains a constant communication with Point Levi on the opposite shore, whence it derives a great part of its provisions. A steam ferry-boat plies every half-hour, making the trip in about ten or fifteen minutes. The navigation also being very properly left free, the river is constanly covered with numerous canoes generally hollowed out from the trunks of trees. The boatmen brave the most tempestuous weather, and though

Prescott Gate, Quebec City, 1839–41, by W. H. Bartlett

often driven several leagues out of their course, are scarcely ever wrecked. Even in winter, when they must encounter blocks of ice with which the channel is encumbered, they contrive with ropes and iron-pointed poles to raise their vessels upon the surface of the masses, and drag them along till they find open water on which to launch it. When this channel is frozen entirely over, the communication becomes still more easy. A line is marked with beacons placed by the Grand Voyer, over which, hay, fireword, with other bulky articles, are transported abundantly and at reduced prices. This advantage occurs only occasionally; but every year the channel between the Isle of Orleans and the northern coast is frozen over, when the produce of that fertile spot, reserved for the occasion, finds a ready conveyance. Formerly milk and vegetables were brought in a frozen state from distant quarters; but now these commodities are procured in abundance from the neighbourhood.

The society of Quebec is more gay and polished than is usual in colonial cities, where the pursuit of wealth forms too often the sole object of the inhabitants. Here, besides merchants, there are a number of British civil and military officers, and a body of French noblesse, living on their domains.[1] These different classes do not, it is said, always thoroughly amalgamate. The French, though often superior in manners and habits, are in some degree disdained by the ruling people, which they do not well brook. Among the English themselves, the chief test of rank is an introduction to the castle,[2] without which strangers will find themselves placed below those whom they would have been classed above in the mother country. The hotels are good, and, after the fashion of the United States, the inmates commonly dine at a *table d' hôte*, which often affords to the visiter the opportunity of meeting with interesting characters. He can, however, if he wishes, have private apartments.

Hugh Murray, *An Historical and Descriptive Account of British America* (Edinburgh: Oliver and Boyd, 1839), Vol. 1, pp. 245-252.

Notes
1. In 1830 about 27 per cent of the population of Quebec City was British.
2. The term "castle" refers to the Château St. Louis in Quebec City, the residence of the governor. The "Château Clique" was a term popularly applied to the governing class in Lower Canada, which was established under the Constitutional Act of 1791. It was composed of the English official element, together with those of the French upper or seigneurial class who were associated with them.

MONTREAL, 1839   32

This description of the city was written by Newton Bosworth, a Baptist minister who served first in Montreal and later in Paris, Upper Canada.

Montreal, the second city in political dignity, but the first in magnitude and commercial importance, in British America, is situated in Latitude 45° 31' North, and Longitude 73° 34' West. Including the suburbs it covers about 1020 acres, although within the fortifications the area did not much exceed 100 acres. Its local advantages for the purposes of trade, give it a decided superiority over every other place in the Province, and its climate, though severe, is more genial than that of Quebec. On approaching it either on the river from below, or in descending from Laprairie, the tall and elegant steeple of the English Church, the massive grandeur of the French Cathedral, the spires of other churches and chapels, the spreading mass of habitations in the suburbs, and the well-built and lofty stores in Commissioner Street, the stranger will be impressed with a very favourable idea of the city he is about to enter. . . .

In the commencément of towns and villages, when no specific plan has been previously arranged, houses and other buildings will be erected where land can be obtained or convenience may dictate, without much regard to regularity or order; and hence, in towns of any considerable standing, we generally find that the earliest streets are crooked and irregular. This may be seen in St. Paul Street in this city, which, by its contiguity to the river, presents great facilities for trade, and, with the space between it and the wharf, would be occupied in preference by men of business. It contains many excellent houses, which would be seen to more advantage, had the street been wider. It reminds one of some of the central streets in London, but without their fog and smoke. . . .

The spirit of local improvement has long been in active and efficient operation, and betrays no symptoms of languor or decline. Those who knew the city seven years ago, and have not seen it since, were they to visit it now, would be surprised at the change, and be scarcely able to recognise the places with which they were once familiar. Beside a multitude of new and elegant houses, in almost every part of the city and suburbs, large spaces and several streets have been considerably improved. The covering of the creek, or rather ditch, an offensive and dangerous nuisance, in Craig Street; the levelling of McGill Street; the improvements in Dalhousie Place, in the French Square, and Notre Dame Street, and of that part of St. Ann Suburbs called Griffin Town, by which a large portion of swampy land has been raised and made available for building, may be adduced as specimens; but the particulars will be more fully noticed in their respective places in the following descriptive account. The recent houses are almost universally built of the greyish limestone which the vicinity of the mountain affords in abundance; the fronts of the same material, hewn and squared; even the new stores and warehouses are finished in the same manner, exhibiting an appearance far more agreeable than those which were constructed of the rough stones, made to fit as far as the mere placing of them could do it, and their interstices filled up with smaller stones and mortar. Many of the houses are large, handsome, and in modern style, and some of them display great taste in design. The prevalent feature is a union of chasteness and elegance in various proportions, with a commendable absence of all meretricious style and ornament. The best houses, and most of the churches, are covered with plates of tin, a far better material for this purpose than the wooden shingles which are frequently used, and though more expensive in the first cost, are cheaper in the end, beside the advantage of safety from fire when buring flakes from neighbouring houses fall upon the roof. . . .

The favourable situation of Montreal enables her to command the trade of a considerable portion of the Lower Province, and the greater part of the Upper. With the United States also, and with Great Britain, an extensive commerce is maintained. Her position, indeed, is such as always to ensure a profitable connection with every part of the continent where business is to be done. By some persons it has been thought, however favourable the situation of Montreal is at present, it would have been better had the city been founded a little lower down the river, so that the difficulty of ascending the Current St. Mary might have been avoided. Should the original design of the Lachine Canal ever be carried into effect, some advantage might result from unloading vessels below the current. The aid of steam navigation, however, by which ships of all burdens may easily be towed up to the city, renders this a consideration of much less importance than it was formerly.

The civil government of Montreal is administered by Justices of the Peace, who are appointed by the Governor of the Province. They are at present forty-six in number, and have power to make certain assessments for defraying the necessary expenses of the city, and to enact and enforce such bye-laws for its regulation and advantage as are not inconsistent with the statutes of the realm. For a short period the municipal affairs of the city were managed by a Mayor and Common Council. An Act passed the Provincial Legislature in 1832, forming Montreal into a Corporation, and transferring the authority from the Magistrates to the corporate body; but in 1836, the Act of Incorporation having expired, the Government again passed into the hands of the Justices of the Peace. The city is represented in the Provincial Parliament by four Members, the East and West Wards into which it is divided, returning two each. The period of service in the House of Assembly is four years. Under the Corporation the city and suburbs were distributed into eight wards, for the more convenient arrangement and dispatch of business. These are East and West Wards, the Wards of St. Ann, St. Joseph, St. Antoine, St. Lawrence, St. Lewis, and St. Mary. Another division of the city may be called the Military, according to which the battalions of militia, which are six in number, are collected from the portions of the city or suburbs in which they reside. . . .

Newton Bosworth, *Hochelaga Depicta; the early history and present state of the City and Island of Montreal* (Montreal: William Greig, 1839), pp. 90-95.

ALEXIS DE TOCQUEVILLE IN LOWER CANADA, 1831

33

Alexis de Tocqueville (1805-1859) was a French liberal politician and writer. He was sent to America by the French government in 1831 to study the penitentiary system. He also visited Lower Canada at this time. On his return to France he published his classic work, Democracy in America.

SOCIETY IN LOWER CANADA

Without comparison, Canada has the greatest similarity to France than any other portion of America we have visited up until now. The banks of the river are perfectly cultivated and covered with houses and villages which are in all, similar to ours. All traces of the wilderness have disappeared and it has been replaced by cultivated fields, steeples, and a population as numerous as in our provinces.

The towns, and Montreal in particular (we have not seen Quebec City), bear a striking resemblance to our provincial towns. The foundation of the population and the large majority of it is French. But it is easy to see that the French are a conquered people. The rich classes belong for the most part to the English race. Although French is the language universally spoken, the majority of the newspapers, notices and even the signs of French merchants are in English. Commercial enterprises are nearly all in their hands. They are really the leading class in Canada. I doubt that this will be the case for long. The clergy and a great part of the classes which are not rich but are enlightened are French. They are beginning to strongly feel their secondary position. The French newspapers I have read wage a constant and lively opposition against the English. Up until now, the people having few needs and intellectual passions and leading a very soft material life, have only caught a very imperfect glimpse of its position as a conquered nation and has provided only a weak support to the enlightened classes. But, for several years, the House of Commons, almost all *Canadian* [i.e. French Canadian], took measures to widely spread education. Everything indicates that the new generation will be different from the present generation. If several years from now the English race does not increase prodigiously by immigration and does not succeed in confining the French to the area they occupy today, the two peoples will find themselves face to face. I cannot believe that they will ever melt together, nor that an indissoluble union can exist between them. I always hope that the French, in spite of the conquest, will one day form by themselves a fine Empire in the New World, more enlightened perhaps, more moral and more content than their fathers. For the present time, this division between races is singularly favourable to the domination of England. . . .

CHARACTERISTICS AND ATTITUDES OF FRENCH CANADIANS

The ideas of these people still seem not very enlightened. However, the people are already conscious that the English are expanding around them at an alarming rate and that they, themselves, are wrong to restrict themselves to one area instead of expanding into unoccupied land. Their jealousy is acutely aroused by the daily arrival of newcomers from Europe. They feel they will be absorbed in the end. They are obviously disturbed by anything that is said on this subject, but they do not clearly see the remedy. French Canadians are too afraid of losing sight of the church steeple. They are not cunning enough. Oh, you are right! But what is to be done? Such are their replies. They evidently feel their position as conquered people and do not count on the benevolence, not exactly, of the government, but more precisely of the English. All their hopes lie with their representatives. They appear to have for them, and particulary for Mr. Neilson,[1] that exalted attachment which oppressed people generally have for their protection. Of Mr. Neilson, they said — with surprise or regret, "However, he is English." Several have appeared to understand very well the need for education and are very much delighted with what has been done in this respect. Over all, French Canadians appear capable of being directed but still incapable of directing themselves. The critical moment is approaching. If twenty years from now, French Canadians have not come out of their apathy, it will be too late for them. Everything indicates that their awakening is approaching. But if the middle and upper classes of the French-Canadian population abandon the lower classes in this effort, and let themselves be led into the English mainstream, the French race in America is lost. This would really be a pity for here are all the elements of a great people. The French of America are to the French of France what the Americans are to the English. They have kept most of the original traits of national character and have mingled them with more morality and more simplicity. Like them, they have thrown off a hoard of prejudices and wrong attitudes which create, and perhaps always will create, the miseries of Europe. In short, they possess all that would be needed to create a remembrance of France in the New World. But will they ever succeed in completely regaining their nationality? This is probable without, unfortunately, being assured. A man of genius who would understand, who would appreciate and who would be able to bring out the national passions of the people would have here a fine role to

Winter scene, Aylmer, Lower Canada, 1839-41, by W. H. Bartlett

play. He would soon become the most powerful man in the colony. But he is not yet anywhere to be seen. . . .

THE HABITANTS

It was the habitants in which we were most interested. It surprises me that this country is so little known in France. Not six months ago I believed, like everyone, that Canada had become completely English. I was going on the account of 1763 which reported the French population to be 60,000. But since then, growth there has been as rapid as in the United States. Today in the province of Lower Canada alone there are 600,000 French descendants. I guarantee that their origin cannot be disputed. They are as French as you and I. They resemble us even better than the Americans of the United States resemble the English. I cannot express what pleasure we felt to find ourselves again amid this population. We felt as if we were at home and everywhere we were received as fellow-countrymen, children of *Old France* as they call it. In my opinion, the epithet is poorly chosen. Old France is in Canada: the new France in France. We rediscovered there, especially in the outlying towns, the former French customs and morals. The villages houses are grouped around a church topped by a weather-cock and a cross ornamented with fleurs-de-lis. The Canadian landowner does not like to isolate himself from his land like his English or American counterpart. These houses are well built, solid on the outside, clean and cared for on the inside. The peasants are well-off and do not pay a penny in taxes. Four times a day, families of hardy parents and strong happy children sit down together at round tables. After dinner some old French song is sung or else some old exploits of the first French in Canada are related: some great sword fights during the time of Montcalm and wars with the English on Sunday. There is leisure and dancing after church services. The curé himself takes part in the festivities as long as they do not degenerate into licentiousness. He is the local oracle, friend and advisor for the popula-tion. Far from being accused of being the partisan of power, the English treat him as a demagogue. The fact is that he is the first to resist oppression and in him the people find their strongest support. Also, Canadians are religious by principle and by political passion. The clergy make up the upper class, not because of laws, but because opinion and morals place them at the head of society. I have seen several of these ecclesiastics and I am still convinced that they are indeed the most distinguished people in the country. They greatly resemble our old French curés. In general, they are cheerful, aimable and well instructed.

Would it not be a temptation to believe that the national character of a people is determined more by the blood from which it came than by political institutions or the nature of a country? Here are Frenchmen who have mingled for years with an English population, who have been subject to the laws of England, who have been more separated from the mother country than if they lived at the Poles. Now! they are still French, characteristic for characteristic. This is true not only for the old but for all, down to the tiny tot spinning his top. Like us, they are lively, alert, intelligent, bantering, fiery, great talkers and extremely difficult to control when their passions are aroused. They are fighters par excellence and prefer action to money. Beside them in this same country are found the stolid English, logicians like the people on the banks of the Thames. They are men of precedents who want the major premise to be established before passing on to the minor premise. They are wise people who think that war is the greatest scourge of the human race, but who, however, wage it as well as others because they have calculated that there are fates worse than death.

Alexis de Tocqueville, *Voyages I. Tocqueville au Bas-Canada*. Introduced by Jacques Vallée (Montreal: Editions du Jour, 1973), pp. 88-89, 100-101, and 107-109.

Note
1. John Neilson (1776 –1848), journalist and politician, member of the House of Assembly from 1818 to 1834, and leader of the popular party in Lower Canada.

34   CLASS STRUCTURE IN LOWER CANADA, 1830

Pierre de Sales Laterrière (1785-1834) studied medicine in Quebec City and in London, England, returning to Quebec City to take over his father's practice. Sympathetic to the views of the reformers, he published A Political and Historical Account of Lower Canada *under the pseudonym "A Canadian" in 1830.*

The ordinary distinctions of rank, as known in the several countries in Europe, exist not in Canada. We have not, in the strict sense of the word, either a *noblesse*, or an *aristocracy* of any kind, though many and important are the distinctions which are really to be found among the people. These divisions or classes, and the habits and manners of each, it is the object of the present chapter to explain.

The most important and marked distinction existing in the country, is of FRENCH and ENGLISH; meaning, by French, all such as were originally, or have, by long dwelling in the country or otherwise, become attached to the French-Canadian habits and language;

Saint James Street, Montreal, 1830, by R. A. Sproule

mcaning, by English, such as are really English, or have, in spite of their continuance in the country, retained a decided predilection for what they believe to be English manners, language, tastes, &c. The civil effects of this division among the people will immediately be seen, when I come to explain the characteristics of the English portion of the population.

The French population, included in the description I have just given, have, by the lapse of years, changed greatly, as regards the various divisions existing among them. The early settlers of these, then wild and desert regions, may easily be conceived not to have been either wealthy, nor nobly born; indeed, we have positive evidence that they were of what are usually termed the lowest—I should say, the most unfortunate classes of society. The soldiers of the French army were oftentimes rewarded by grants of lands in Canada; the adventurous, idle, and desperate went out in search of golden fortunes there; and to these, for the purpose of providing them worthy partners, the government dispatched a cargo of women. When, by the combined endeavours of these various persons, the country became somewhat populous and thriving, various families connected with the *noblesse* of France were induced to become settlers in these new territories, by large grants of land, and the donatives of various important privileges. Thus *noble* families were mingled with the Canadian population.

So long as the country was under the dominion of France, the *noblesse* formed the leading people of the country; they constituted the fashionable society in Quebec, and imitated, at the Château St. Louis,[1] as far as their means permitted, the splendour and ceremony of the Court of Versailles. When the country was taken by the English, the greater part of the nobles departed: some, however, remained; and being well received by the English governors, and treated with distinction on account of their rank, they still shone, though with diminished splendour, amid the circles of Quebec. The forms of the age of Louis XIV were in some degree preserved in this distant land, after they had disappeared from the country which gave them birth; and, under the fostering care of the government, protracted for a short period the date of their existence. Causes, however, were in operation, which eventually destroyed this lingering influence of the nobility.

The English introduced among the population a spirit of traffic; they taught them to appreciate the advantages of individual wealth, and to feel that a man might be of importance, even though not descended from a noble race. The English traders spread themselves over the country, bartered and trafficked with the inhabitants, introducing new articles of luxury, and creating a demand for the various productions of the country. The bourgeoisie, or *ignoble* inhabitants of the towns, caught the spirit — laboured, and laboured successfully, to accumulate wealth for themselves; and, being a frugal and a prudent race, they quickly found themselves possessed of fortunes more than sufficient to enable them to cope with the broken-down *noblesse* around them. They, therefore, immediately began to compete with this fading generation, both in political and social life. The nobles themselves, preserving, in undiminished vigour, the absurd and baneful feelings universally engendered where aristocratic distinctions exist, looked with disdain upon the occupation of a merchant. To obtain their own livelihood, they considered a degradation: To live upon the labour of others, they deemed an honourable prerogative. In the present state of affairs, however, they possess no power to wring from other men the means of splendour or subsistence; being idle, they consequently became wretchedly poor.

Pierre de Sales Laterrière, *A Political and Historical Account of Lower Canada* (London: Marsh and Miller, 1830), pp. 114–116.

Note
1. The residence of the governor until 1834, when it was destroyed by fire.

---

35   SOCIAL LIFE IN LOWER CANADA: AMURY GIROD, 1835

Born in France, Amury Girod came to Lower Canada about 1828. A reformer, he was one of the delegates to the mass meeting at Saint-Charles on October 23, 1837. When the Rebellion of 1837 broke out, he went to Saint-Eustache as general-in-chief, but left when the troops arrived on December 14. Four days later he was recognized at Point-aux-Trembles and committed suicide to avoid capture.

Girod was the author of Notes diverses sur le Bas-Canada, *which was written to inform the British government and members of Parliament about the state of Lower Canada. In discussing grievances, he contended that over-government was a more serious evil than neglect, since it sapped initiative. He attributed the rapid development of new communities and economic enterprises in the United States to the fact that people in that country were left to manage their own local affairs.*

I should say that I do not plan to discuss the so-called social life in Canada. What is called society elsewhere, does not exist here. The population of Lower Canada is divided into French, English, Scottish, British and American. If by social connection and relationship one means something more than a wild party, a ball where new dresses are paraded, one will have to agree with me that these sections of society in Canada are separated from one another as were in days gone by, the castes of Egypt, or rather, like the *Neri* and the *Bianchi* in Florence.

French Canadians have one trait in common, I shall make use of the statement made by an Englishman who spoke of this trait in 1812, that is to say, in times of danger, "their military spirit, so often displayed before their connection with Great Britain, came to the forefront each time danger was renewed and this same devotion to king and country which impelled their fathers to accomplish feats of glory is not lacking in the sons. The French-Canadian genius, customs, and way of life prepare them for military life. They like action, pomp and parade. They live with little, and take on difficult tasks. They withstand the greatest strain with admirable strength."

The French Canadians are subdivided into those of the old and new school. The first have all the urbanity and amiable qualities of their fathers in the century of Louis XIV. Add to this, however, large doses of geniality which the ex-mother country never had. Amidst them, the old *régime* will not be attacked with impunity. But there is in this sweet sobriety neither pride nor presumption. There is seen that purity of morals, that strict honesty, that real hospitality and that good humour, which on the continent of Europe, in England and in the cities of the neighbouring states, are unfortunately known only through books. In all classes of Canadian society, there is a great attachment to the French name. This is seen even in their absurdities, in that desire to know if someone has run across a hamlet in France having such and such a name, in that desire to know whether Canadian styles resemble in some way the styles of Paris. But it is the attachment of an emancipated son to his unaware father whom he cannot prevent himself from loving, although he can no longer respect him; since he abandoned him in childhood to the mercy of the elements and the pity of the wolves of the wilderness. It is a social attachment. The government of Louis XV broke all ties of a political attachment.

In the class of Canadians which I am discussing is found what one would search in vain to find in the majority of families of the old regime, that old amiability and geniality combined with the candour and more useful learnings of modern time.

Canadians of the new school are a completely different lot. Lively, in search of education, a little hot-headed, a little less polite, but more frank, scornful of all the little nothings which made the society of the *salons* so charming. They are almost exclusively given to the politics of their country. I have never met men more disposed to submitting themselves to justice and reason, nor people more resolved to resist the oppression and arrogance of the *maîtres*. These people will be the firm support of a *just* government which comes to them from England, but the Minister on Downing Street would do well not to persist in sending them incompetent or dishonest men who perpetuate abuses and oppression.

The country people, the *habitants*, as they are ordinarily called, are indeed men of geniality on all occasions, intelligent and amiable. They present a striking contrast to the sly-expressioned, ill-manner English or Scottish immigrants. They are not educated, but I shall discuss that point at another time. Wherever Canadians have not been corrupted by proximity to the towns or connection with the British population, a more honest, more gentle people cannot be found. But every year come shiploads of immigrants, that is to say, the poor who have been exiled from England. They bring with them the whole civilization of the mother country: tricks, debauchery, and fights. I fear this contagion more than the ruin of anything else. It is hardly possible to better describe this respectable class of Canadian society than did a bitter enemy of the cause of this people. "In general," he says, "the Canadians in the country are very religious and peaceful, except when their property rights are in danger. They are honest, hospitable, polite, discerning and not at all susceptible to the extreme emotions which too often influence the multitude when they are skilfully aroused. It is not to be feared that they would ever want to deviate from the path of loyalty."

It is noteworthy that the author [of this quote] writes these words in a laudatory work on the administration of Sir James Craig and of the Count Dalhousie which presents the country in a state nearing revolt.

I have also observed that Canadians generally are a religious people, devoted to their clergy, tolerant towards the Protestants, but distrusting of whoever is not of their church. They hold with the preservation of their ancient customs, laws, institutions and of their language. It is to be regretted that Great Britain nearly always has a colonial secretary who is so thoroughly ignorant of the real situation in these provinces that she cannot profit from such an arrangement, in order to assure the loyalty of the colonies. If ever there were another war with the United States, I am certain that the latter would benefit from it, and I am sure that the Canadians would never want to have anything to do with the Union without having their nationality guaranteed. But if the system of *mad* oppression, which the delegates of British power exercise in this colony continues, I fear that the United States can soon take possession of the right bank of the St. Lawrence without one Canadian rising up to give them chase, provided that they are guaranteed their nationality.

Amury Girod, *Notes diverses sur le Bas-Canada* (Village Debartzch: Imprimerie de J.-P. Boucher-Belleville, 1835), pp. 22-23.

---

36   THE HABITANTS: HUGH MURRAY, 1839

In his compendium of information on British North America, An Historical and Descriptive Account of British America, *Hugh Murray includes this account of the French Canadians.*

The *habitants*, at the time of the conquest, formed almost the whole of the European population. They had occupied the best lands along the banks of the St. Lawrence, between Quebec and Montreal; a considerable extent of those upon the Richelieu; and a small space on the Chaudière, the Yamaska, the St. Maurice and other tributaries of the great river, as well as a detached settlement on the fertile shores of the Detroit. These tracts had been granted to persons of distinction and to favourites, usually in large blocks, which . . . they held under the title of seigneurs. But it accorded not with their habits to clear and cultivate for themselves grounds covered with an unbroken forest; nor would the task be undertaken by farmers on the terms of an ordinary lease. The proprietors were therefore obliged to make them over, in small lots, under the feudal title of fiefs, to hard-working men, who, on receiving this permanent interest, were willing to encounter the toil. The annual payment or quit-rent is in general exceedingly small, amounting on some properties to only 10s. a year, with a bushel of wheat and two fowls. The seigneur has, besides, certain feudal claims; a tithe on fish, mill-dues, and, more especially, payments on sale or transference, which in some cases amount to a fifth of the purchase-money.

The occupants of these fiefs or farms, under the burdens now specified, are virtual proprietors of the soil, which they cultivate with their own hands, aided by their families. They are described as a particularly contented, industrious, and amiable race of people; and the lots, though much subdivided in the course of succession, are still sufficient to maintain them in simple plenty. They till their lands with diligence, though without skill, having scarcely adopted any of the modern improvements. Their study is to produce from the farm everything they need; not only the whole of their food, but their candles, soap and even sugar. From flax of their own raising, too, and the wool of their own sheep, they are enabled to manufacture almost every article of clothing. Their houses, though generally built of wood and only one story high, are whitewashed, and tolerably commodious. A partition in the middle separates the kitchen from the principal apartment, at one end of which are the bedrooms. There is a garden which, though in a somewhat rude and straggling state, and cultivated by the females only, yields a comfortable supply of the more common fruits and vegetables.

The personal appearance of the *habitants* is peculiar. They are tall, thin, and, from exposure to the climate, almost as dark as the Indians. They have thin lips and often aquiline noses, with small, dark, and lively eyes. Many of the girls are pretty oval-faced brunettes, with fine eyes, good teeth, and glossy locks. The dress is nearly after the old fashion of the French peasantry. The men wear the *capot*, a large gray coat or surtout, covering nearly the whole body, and tied with a girdle of brilliant colours. On the legs they have moccasins, and on the head a straw hat in summer, and a red bonnet in winter. The hair is still tied in a long queue behind. The women wear short jackets or bedgowns (mantelets), with petticoats distinct, and sometimes a different colour, and caps instead of bonnets; a mode of dress formerly common in Scotland, and not yet wholly disused. They have long waists, and sometimes the hair tied behind a large club. At church, or other occasions of full dress, they adopt the English fashion, but display a much greater variety of showy colours. Hair-powder is sometimes worn, and beet-root employed as rouge; but both in their dress and houses, they are perfectly clean.

The *habitants* are frugal and moderate in their ordinary diet, which mostly consists of different kinds of soup. They have, however, their *jours gras*, or great feast-days, particularly before and after Lent, when large companies assemble, and the board is spread with every delicacy which their larder can afford. The table groans beneath immense turkey pies, huge joints of beef, mutton, and pork, followed by a profusion of fruit-puddings. Extraordinary justice is said to be done to these viands, as well as to the rum which follows; but the younger members of the company are soon roused by the sound of the violin; and the dancing, of which they are passionately fond, engages them till a late hour. Weddings, above all, are celebrated by a mighty concourse of friends and acquaintances. Twenty or thirty of the country carriages bring in parties to witness the ceremony, which is followed by feasts and dances not unfrequently prolonged for several days. The young people, however, have a somewhat rude method of expressing their opinion of an unequal union, especially if arising from the relative age of the parties. They assemble at night in large bodies, sounding various discordant instruments, horns, drums, bells, kettles, accompanied by loud shouts; and a contribution to the church or some charitable purpose is indispensable to obtain a respite from this jocular persecution. The short summer is necessarily spent in almost unremitting labour; but when ice and snow have covered the ground, the gay season begins, and in their carioles or little chaises on steel runners, which pass swiftly over the frozen surface, they visit their neighbours, and spend much time in social intercourse.

The Canadian French, like their forefathers, profess the Roman Catholic religion with much zeal, and in a manner which occasionally approaches superstition. The roads are marked by crosses erected at the site; their houses are filled with little pictures of the Madonna and child, waxen images of saints, and of the crucifixion; and there is a profuse expenditure of holy water and candles. They reluctantly establish their dwelling beyond hearing of the church bells, and on Sundays the attendance is crowded. They have, however, those inadequate notions as to the sanctity of that day, which are general in Catholic countries. When worship is over, the remainder is devoted, without reserve, to amusement. ''Sunday,'' it is said, ''is to them their day of gayety; there is then an assemblage of friends and relations; the parish-church collects together all whom they know, with whom they have relations of business or pleasure; the young and old, men and women, clad in their best garments, riding their best horses, driving in their gayest *calèches*, meet there for purposes of business, love, and pleasure. The young *habitant*, decked out in his most splendid finery, makes his court to the maiden whom he has singled out as the object of his affections; the maiden, exhibiting in her adornment every colour of the rainbow, there hopes to meet her chevalier; the bold rider descants upon and gives evidence of the merits of his unrivalled pacer; and in winter the powers of the various horses are tried in sleigh or cariole racing; in short, Sunday is the grand fête.'' Even the violin and the dance in the evening are not considered unsuitable. Notwithstanding these customs, the religious spirit of the Canadians appears sincere, and is attended with great benefits. Their general conduct is inoffensive and praiseworthy. Crimes of an atrocious description, as murder and violent assaults upon the person, scarcely ever occur. Property is perfectly safe, both from the thief and the robber; the doors of the houses stand open, and all sorts of goods are exposed without any precaution. They scarcely ever engage in those furious personal conflicts which, among the Americans of English descent, are often carried on with such violence; they know neither duelling, boxing, nor gouging. On the contrary, they mutually treat each other with all the ceremonious politeness of the French school. One of the first things taught to a child is to speak decorously, to bow or curtsey to its elders or to strangers. This politeness is not accompanied with any degree of insincerity or servility, above which last they are completely raised by their independent situation. They are said to be generous in relieving those in distress, liberal and courteous to all who have any claim on their hospitality. The custom of parents and children living together, often to the third generation, in the same house, marks a mild and friendly temper. The only form under which hostile passions are vented is that of litigation, to which they are immoderately addicted, being favoured by the comparative cheapness of law. . . .

The *habitants* are not a stirring, enterprising, or improving race. They tread in the steps of their forefathers, following the same routine, and with difficulty adopting the most obvious improvements of modern husbandry. Although extensive tracts lie in their immediate neighbourhood unoccupied, they resign them to the English and Americans, and have scarcely at all extended the range of their original settlement. Even their amiable qualities tend to retain them in this stationary condition; to which we may add their social disposition, their attachment to their kindred, their church, and the rites of their religion. They feel as if in leaving these things they would leave all. Their range of information has hitherto been very limited; and their priests, it has been alleged, by no means favour the diffusion among them even of the first elements of education; so that the majority of the adults cannot even read or write. But the legislature have lately made great exertions to improve them in this respect, and it is hoped that the rising generation will be more enlightened. . . .

Hugh Murray, *An Historical and Descriptive Account of British America* (Edinburgh: Oliver and Boyd, 1839), Vol. 2, pp. 52-60.

THE PEOPLE OF THE TOWNSHIPS: JOSEPH BOUCHETTE, 1832   37

Joseph Bouchette was appointed Surveyor-General of Lower Canada in 1804. His important topographical work, The British Dominions in North America, *from which this excerpt is taken, was published in 1832.*

The people of the townships form a distinct class of themselves, and are strikingly contrasted with the French-Canadian peasantry of the province. The tenure of their lands, their language, and their habits, are essentially, their laws partially, different from those of the seigneurial population, and assimilate in many respects with those of the neighbouring settlements of the United States. The origin of this similitude may be traced to the early stages of the colonization of the eastern townships, when the settlers were almost exclusively, if not altogether, natives of the adjacent country, and emigrants from the New York, Vermont and New England States. The numerous class of British and Irish emigrants that subsequently took up crown lands in the townships, strangers in general to the mode of clearing and cultivating new lands, were naturally prone to imitate those who had preceded them in these important operations, and the American settler, proverbially dexterous and active in removing forests with the axe, thus became the model of the European emigrant. This imitation was not long confined to the mode of converting a wilderness into corn fields, but soon extended to the plan of building their houses, dividing and tilling their farms, &c. The domestic economy of the establishment and the usages of the new settlers thus gradually approximated to those of the old, and although there are now some exceptions, the manners and customs of the people of the townships, generally, bear a close analogy to the manners and customs of the Americans.

The composition of the township population is multifarious, and the inhabitants of each class might rank, according to their numbers, in the following order: first Americans, then Irish, Scotch, English, Dutch, and Germans. We have already taken an opportunity of speaking of the industry which characterizes the people of that part of the province, and it may be here observed, that the description given in the preceding pages of the ease and comforts of the Canadian peasantry is not inapplicable to the townships, though, perhaps, to a more limited extent, from the comparative infancy of the settlements. Neither do the township inhabitants yield to the French Canadians in point of loyalty; all feel equally attached to their king, their government, and their institutions.

The different elements of the population being, as we have remarked, very numerous, the same unity of feeling, customs, and character can scarcely be expected to prevail to the same degree as in the French settlements; but it is gratifying, however, to observe that there exists in the townships but little, if any, of that party-spirit, religious or political, which links one set of men against another, and destroys the harmony of society, whilst it tends to paralyse the progress of new, and effect the prosperity of old settlements.

The population of the towns is distinguished by few peculiarities that are not common to the inhabitants of populous places. Here we find the same gradations of rank, the same assumptions on the one hand, and denials of superiority on the other, that are incident to similar communities. The circumstance of the two chief places of the provinces being garrison towns, serves also to give a certain complexion to society, which is peculiar to the *art militaire*, whilst it, at the same time, contributes to the outward gayety, at least, of the place. However remote from the vortex of the *haut ton* on this side of the Atlantic, the higher circles are by no means strangers to the delicacies, etiquette, and refinements of European society; and by the agreeable union of French and English manners, that forms so peculiar a feature of the society in Canada, a degree of vivacity prevails, which holds a medium course between the austerity of English reserve and the ebullitions of French rhapsody.

Joseph Bouchette, *The British Dominions in North America; or a Topographical and Statistical Description of Lower and Upper Canada, New Brunswick, Nova Scotia, the Islands of New Foundland, Prince Edward, and Cape Breton* (London: Longman, 1832), Vol. 1, pp. 416–417.

---

38   JUSTICE IN LOWER CANADA: ISIDORE LEBRUN, 1833

Isidore Lebrun was a French literary figure and teacher who, following a visit to Canada, wrote a book on his observations in 1833.

At the session of September 1831, in Montreal, the grand jury admitted 34 indictments and rejected 18: there were 23 persons convicted. The business of the following October quarter was as follows: 8 convictions, 37 bills of indictment submitted to the grand jury, of which 13 were for assault and battery; 10 bills for petty larceny, 4 for brothels; 10 trials prepared; 5 bills rejected; 25 accused granted bail to appear at the next session, 16 for vice; 14 police reports confirmed and 20 prisoners freed. At the February 1832 term, 38 bills were introduced, 10 rejected; the court decided on 31 cases. The grand jury indicted 53 individuals and rendered 11 acquittals; the petty jury found 28 of 49 accused to be guilty. A trimestrial session at Quebec made only 14 convictions, the most serious for larceny, at 6 months in prison and a whipping. At last September's session, an assault (battery) was punished by 6 months imprisonment and a guarantee of good conduct for 3 years, the convicted man paying 100 louis and each of his two guarantors 50 louis.

Theft of an article valuing less than 20 shillings is petty larceny. The law also distinguishes theft committed in a ship from theft committed in an occupied house. The

Parish Church of Notre Dame, Montreal, 1839–41, by W. H. Bartlett

penalty for libel or defamation of 2 civil servants was 15 pounds sterling and imprisonment until payment. Swindling, larceny and attempted theft of government property —3 months of hard labour. Issuing a counterfeit American bank-note—6 months in prison. For theft from a shop—12 months, and for theft from an occupied house —1 month, and 25 pounds sterling bail for housebreaking and personal assault. Conspiracy to deprive a woman of seigniorial lands of which she is the proprietor—4 and 2 months in prison, and a fine of 10 pounds. Six months with the pillory for attempting to induce a soldier to desert. The death penalty for burglary; for theft of personal property from an individual, and theft similarly defined, 1 month in prison and 39 strokes of the whip after exposure to public view. Perpetual banishment for theft of personal property from a shop. Three months in prison for keeping a house of prostitution. Twenty shillings fine to the King's coffers for assault and battery of a person who received no compensation. Sometimes, on the jury's recommendation, or in response to the offender's plea for mercy, the court mitigates the penalty. The court also takes into consideration either a previous long imprisonment or attenuating circumstances: the penalty for the theft of a sheep has been restricted to 3 months in prison. More often, animal theft is punishable by death. Issuing counterfeit currency brings 12 months in prison and one hour in the pillory.

Isidore Lebrun, *Tableau statistique et politique des deux Canada* (Quebec: Neilson et Cowan, 1833), pp. 440–441.

View of Notre Dame Street, Montreal, 1830, by R. A. Sproule

---

39   RELIGIOUS GROUPS IN LOWER CANADA, MONTREAL, AND QUEBEC CITY, 1831

POPULATION OF LOWER CANADA: 553,134.

	Lower Canada	Montreal	Quebec City
Roman Catholic	412,717	43,773	36,179
Church of England	34,620	5,888	5,582
Church of Scotland	15,069	3,643	2,181
Presbyterian	7,810	1,005	163
Methodist	7,018	517	337
Baptist	2,461	105	14
Jewish	107	52	3
Other	5,577	30	23
Not given	67,755	—	6

Census of Canada, Vol. 4, p. 109.

---

40   THE ROLE OF THE CLERGY IN LOWER CANADA, 1833

Le Canadien, August 30, 1833.

There is, therefore, nothing, absolutely nothing, which could separate the people from their clergy. Would it be fear of reform? From all parts of the Province, we hear nothing but unanimous praise with respect to the clergy. Unlike most European priesthoods, it has not had the misfortune to be overwhelmed with possessions and wealth, so incompatible with its institution, and, consequently, it does not fear losing them. The current revenue of the clergy is generally only sufficient to allow, with thrift, decent comfort and nothing more. If some parish priests report large incomes, we know that they are applied to acts of benevolence, and it is largely due to this source that the southern shore in the district of Quebec possesses St. Anne's College, the Trois-Rivières district Nicolet College, the southern part of the Montreal district St. Hyacinthe College and Chambly College, and that the northern part of the Montreal district will soon have Assumption College. The clergy, individually or collectively, pays the fees and expenses of several students in our different colleges. . . . We doubt that any other pious people in the world receives as much for what it gives, not even our neighbours in the United States. We also declare, and we do not fear contradiction, that Canadian patriots are determined that their clergy conserve the secular existence it has today, and they would be in a most unhappy situation if they found themselves unable to continue to protect this existence. . . .

Woe unto those who would use time-worn doctrines to cause war between two groups of men still united by the most sacred and precious bonds, and whose union doubles the strength of the Canadian cause and assures its success.

THE CLERGY AND POLITICS, 1835   41

L'Ami du Peuple was founded in Montreal in 1832 by Pierre-Edouard Leclerc and John Jones. Real influence, however, was exercised by the Catholic church. Its stated purpose was to promote truth, virtue, and morality. It spoke out strongly against the Patriotes. This excerpt is taken from the issue of 17 January 1835.

. . . Nothing then, could be more out of place, and I dare say more scandalous, than for a priest to make use of the sacred functions of his ministry in order to further, even with the finest intentions in the world, purely political views. The Bishop's duty would be then, to severely reprimand such a priest. What shows that this view is founded in reason is that the masses, when not subjected to any influence, are, in these circumstances, generally much better judges than they are commonly believed to be. They feel that their lack of education does not permit them to speak. However, their common sense is often so excellent that it could be said that the difference in education is in their favour.

The priest, in the above situation, is not strictly speaking for any one policy nor for any one government. To put in another way, he is for all policies and for all governments. Since all authority comes from God by whatever route, his duty, which is well laid down by St. Paul and further by [Jesus Christ] himself, is to recognize the authority of the day and to submit to it in all that is just and reasonable. As the apostle said "*rationabile obsequium vestrum*" and this without trouble or tumult, in a word without extinguishing the eternal flame. . . .

. . . This established without argument I hope, I now ask why an educated, moderate priest who has been meditating in silence for a long time on the nature and course of events, could not form his own opinion and could not pass his opinion on to some of his friends in society. Why could he not be permitted to say, for example, that we have committed an unforgivable blunder in our latest elections, the consequences of which can be most disastrous for the whole country and particularly for the people, on whom nearly anything can be imposed if they are deluded by the illusive promise of exemption from all social burdens. A particular example of this is the tithe which is being stirred up all over the province. It is then shrewdly made to appear to the farmers that priests only oppose actions, the 92 Resolutions, for example, through fear of losing their rich revenues. It was in this way by being deprived of the means by which to live, the clergy in France began to be and were successfully driven out.

Why could a priest who knew that a candidate had principles that were harmful to the country not expose him as such to his parishioners and to other voters who did not know him. Would it be excusable for this priest who knew of some plot against the state not to reveal it under the pretext that priests should not involve themselves in worldly affairs. . . .

---

42   THE CLERGY IN LOWER CANADIAN POLITICS: IGNACE BOURGET, 1837

Ignace Bourget was born in Lower Canada in 1779. He was educated at the Quebec Seminary and ordained a priest in 1822. On the founding of the diocese of Montreal in 1836, he was appointed its first vicar-general, becoming Bishop of Montreal in 1840. Although in sympathy with many of the Patriotes' ideas, Bourget attempted to remain neutral during the events surrounding the rebellions, urging his fellow clergy to speak the truth without fear of consequences, as he does in this letter to a priest at St. Charles, Father Blanchet.

. . . You will always be welcome to express your opinions.

But here are the thoughts which occur to me concerning the intervention of the clergy which you believe necessary for the redress of our grievances.

In this new step, we will, of necessity, have to become involved in politics; we will have to decide if the Legislative Council is a public nuisance, if the Constitution is no longer good and if it should be changed. . . . Now, are we entitled to judge in such a matter? Would we not be acting contrary to the wishes of the Patriotes who would like to remove us completely from the political scene? We find in our Holy Books that one of the duties of the people is to never resist the established authority of God. . . .

Some people claim that this step will stir up a hatred of the clergy, and that this pastoral letter will not bring about any good. Supposing this to be true, are there not urgent circumstances under which men must be told the truth even though it will necessarily shock them? Our Lord knew very well that he would not make the Scribes and the Pharisees believe in him by telling them that he was the Son of God, and he even knew that his confession of divinity would bring upon him a most ignominious death. However, you know as well as I how freely he told the truth; and how zealously he inveighed against their vices, without fear of compromising the interests of his newly-formed Church. *He made us understand by his example, that we must never fear the persecution of men when it is a question of showing them their duty,* and that it is not by cowardly silence that respect for the honour of religion is attracted, but rather by a truly saintly freedom in preaching, irrespective of the subsequent response. . . .

Rapport de l'archiviste de la province de Québec, 1945-1946, quoted in Léon Pouliot, *Monseigneur Bourget et son temps* (Montreal: Beauchemin, 1955-1956), Vol. I, pp. 137-139.

THE BENEFITS OF TWO LANGUAGES, 1831   43

Le Canadien, October 12, 1831.

. . . During the last session of parliament as noted previously, the elected representatives from the Eastern Townships initiated a petition to the King demanding the reintroduction of French laws in the townships. It has been learned that at the next session of parliament they will benefit from a recent act of the Imperial Parliament regarding this matter. These sensible and reflective people are not unaware that the existence of the old laws lead to the growth of the language in which they are written and explained. Their lawyers, notaries and judges should learn them. Since they want to keep them, they should have their children who will join the law professions learn them. It would even seem that thought is being given to introducing the study of French into their schools. The following lines appeared in the *St. Francis Courier* on the fourth of this month:—

"Another thing I recommend is the teaching of French, at least in the academies and village schools for the present and the gradual introduction of French into each English school in the province . . . . I am of the opinion that a knowledge of French is a necessity for each person living in Lower Canada where a large proportion of the population speaks this language. The ability to communicate freely with the French-speaking population will assist in the disappearance of the prejudices which have unfortunately existed for too long among us. It is not only in Lower Canada that I believe a knowledge of French is necessary, but in the whole country. It is very much in use in high society in all countries and it is used as much as perhaps any other language in the world."

These are the words of the people who are portrayed to us as wanting to destroy our laws and our customs. The rational portion of the English population interested in the general welfare of the country is ridding itself of prejudices. A portion of the population interested in getting rid of the two divisions in the Canadian population knew how to inspire them. They want to make common cause with the people who planted the tree of civilization in this country. They want to join their destiny to their own destiny, a sure way of creating a happy strong people. Another policy for its part would tend only to cause a civil war between the two families which would weaken them. Both would become the certain prey of a common enemy.

The reconciliation that has taken place between the two populations since the last act of the representatives has made the objections to a close union between them disappear. The existence among one of the populations of a system of laws unknown to the other population was a definite cause of the antipathy between them. Fortunately, the new came to have an equal aversion to these laws and are now demanding the old laws with some slight modifications that their particular situation requires. This has happened to such an extent that soon we will have throughout the country uniformity in laws and the administration of justice. It is to be assumed that the changes to be made in the laws for the townships will be such as to be applicable in the seigneuries. This is to be hoped. Only language will be different in Lower Canada. But, this will only be the case for the masses, and they never come into contact. Communication from one part of a vast country to the other is always made by the prominent classes of society. In their education, these classes will place the language of Shakespeare and that of Racine on an equal footing. Out of interest and need they will do what other countries have done for pleasure. Are those who aim to destroy our language unable to see the consequent benefit the country would receive from the use of both of the languages most generally spoken today? There is almost no country in the world, no matter how distant, with which we could not maintain relations, with English *and* French. Not to mention literature and science. These two languages open to us the treasures of the two richest and most beautiful literatures which have ever existed or will exist for some time. A fine, great idea for a civilizer or founder of an empire would be that which would introduce the usage of the two queens of modern literature, and posterity would praise his undertaking. By what distorted logic could anyone wish to thwart such an idea, when by force of circumstance it already happens to be an established fact?

44   SCHOOLS AND STUDENTS IN LOWER CANADA, 1828-1844

Year	Number of Schools	Number of Students
1828	325	11,679
1829	465	18,410
1830	987	41,791
1831	1,282	45,203
1832	1,038	41,377
1833	1,075	45,158
1834	1,273	50,230
1835	1,372	53,377

Louis-Philippe Audet, *Histoire de l'enseignement au Québec, 1680-1840* (Montreal: Holt, Rinehart et Winston, 1971), Vol. 1, p. 387.

45   SCHOOLS IN LOWER CANADA, 1835

The following excerpt is taken from a school reader published in Lower Canada in 1835 and intended for use in English-speaking elementary schools.

LESSON FORTY FIRST

Education

Schools have long been established at Quebec and Montreal, and several other places, (for the education of the sons and daughters of the wealthy and the higher classes of society), but it is only a few years since the general establishment of schools, for the education of the poor as well as the rich, received much encouragement from the government. For several years past, however, the subject of general education has engaged much of the attention of the Provincial Parliament. In all of the townships which are sufficiently settled, primary and elementary schools are established in each neighbourhood by government and sufficient money is granted (usually about twenty pounds,) from the revenue of the province, to support the school nearly the whole year, without any other tax upon the people, than boarding the teacher and providing fuel for the school room. (Schools are also established in most of the parishes of the seigniories), and are encouraged in like manner. According to the return of 1831, the whole number of elementary schools in the province was 1,099. Besides these there is a considerable number of (academies, convents and colleges) in which the higher branches are taught, and most of which are in part supported by (annual grants made by the Provincial Parliament.) The academies have usually received from 100 to 200 pounds each, annually. The whole number of these institutions in 1831 was (38) Of these nine are colleges, about 20 convents, and the remainder academies. There are three colleges at Montreal, one at Chambly, one at St. Hyacinth, one at Nicolet, two at Quebec, and one at St. Anne in the county of Kamouraska. Of the convents six are extensive (nunneries) situated in large towns. The others are established in different parts of the province for (the education of females,) and are generally under the government and instruction of two or three nuns. All of the above (colleges and convents,) with the exception of M'gill college at Montreal, which has not yet formally gone into operation, are (under the direction of Roman Catholics,) and the instruction is generally given in the (French language.) The academies are mostly in the townships, and under the direction of the protestants. In the townships reading, writing, arithmetic, English grammar and geography are taught in the elementary schools, and all the children have an opportunity to obtain a competent knowledge of the useful branches of education.

Zadock Thompson, *Geography and History of Lower Canada* (Stanstead and Sherbrooke, Lower Canada: Walton and Gaylord, 1835), pp. 60-61.

EDUCATION IN LOWER CANADA, 1832   **46**

La Minerve, 3 May 1832 (a letter to the editor).

The Editor,
We have come to a stage where that education which seemed to prosper as it became

Ice bridge, between Quebec City and Point Lévis, Lower Canada, 1831, by Lieutenant-Colonel Cockburn

established, is going to lapse into a stage of inactivity and decadence. While the government still distributes huge sums over the entire province for its maintenance, the purpose is not to perfect education but only to maintain and encourage it, and it is left up to the inhabitants to carry it to perfection. Indeed, under the new regulations, children are excluded from the schools as soon as they reach the age of twelve; the poor no longer have the privilege of being educated without payment) the number of pupils will decline; the inevitable result of this arrangement will be that schools will not exist in such large numbers as before. Young people who, until now, were free to go to school until they were adequately educated, will find themselves obliged to leave their studies at the time when they give promise of making the most rapid progress. Then they will not have enough ability or knowledge to practise what they have learned and to acquire new skills on their own. Will children be suited to some employment or will they subsequently be able to fend for themselves in all their private business? Our experience tells us, ''No.'' Indeed, what will be their education? They will know how to read and write, but they will read without understanding what they read; they will be incapable of writing a word correctly and with an understanding of what they write. They will leave the schools without any taste for study because they will not understand anything about it; and such an education will soon be lost from their memory.

If the Canadian people persist in their unpardonable indifference to education, we should then expect to see education stagnate and degenerate in this imperfect state, and the largesse of the Legislature prove fruitless for the province. It is up to you, ''habitants,'' to leave no stone unturned in conquering this dislike of the sciences which sometimes makes us contemptible in the eyes of foreigners, and in coming out of this ignorance in which our ancestors, who did not possess the educational advantages we have today, lived. To this end, if people want the funds advanced by the government to be turned to their best use, it is vital that they establish an institution in every parish or at least in every county where children could go after having learned reading and writing in the lower schools, to take a complete Grammar course, to get some idea of Literature, History and Geography; to study carefully Arithmetic and other sciences which could be taught there. It could probably be said, as indeed it has, that there are enough colleges where our youth can receive all the education desirable. It is true that we have colleges where education prospers, and which provide the province with a great number of literate young men; but these proposed institutions will be much less expensive, and studies will not be as long there as in the colleges where Latin is a necessity.

A Teacher

Note
1. The education acts of 1829 and 1832 were quite similar. The Act of 1829 gave the Parliament of Lower Canada authority over education. The government agreed to pay half the cost of a school building to a maximum of £50; to grant a salary of £20 a year to teachers; and to give a grant of ten shillings for each poor child receiving free instruction, provided that there were at least twenty and not more than fifty pupils. The Act of 1832 laid down the duties of school trustees and inspectors. The new legislation also specified the duties of teachers, certificates of teaching competence, the length of the school year, the number of pupils, teachers' compensation, roll calls, official inspections, attendance books, local regulations, and dismissal of teachers for incompetence or improper behaviour. Government grants were made not only to public schools but to all categories of schools then in existence: royal schools, *fabrique* schools, and the private schools operated by religious orders.

HOW TO REMEDY THE SITUATION IN EDUCATION, 1835   47

A letter from M. Ducharme, a priest from Ste. Thérèse, presented to the Legislative Assembly by Louis H. Lafontaine, deputy from Terrebonne, 14 December 1835.

. . . Would it not be right for the teachers who are responsible for teaching in the villages to receive a higher salary than that received by the ones on the coasts, and at the same time require them to give their students some knowledge of geography, history, etc. The assumption would be that these teachers had a more complete education than that of certain good ladies who are barely capable of providing an adequate and sometimes very mediocre education at the elementary level, but who receive, nonetheless, the same wages as the teachers who have passed a course. It certainly seems that the trying work of a teacher is considered by many people too lowly for a well-educated person to devote himself to.

Requiring of the teachers six hours of school daily is too much for their health and the health of the children, particularly in periods of extreme heat when you have about sixty children among whom several are very poorly dressed. If you are not convinced of what I am saying, just go into these schools one hour after the children have assembled and you will see that the air is so filled with rank vapours that you can hardly bear it one hour after they leave. This point deserves attention.

If I dared voice my opinion on the best way to awaken interest in education or rather to rouse our residents' attention, I would say that nothing would be more effective than subjecting them to some contribution. They would not miss the opportunity of saying: "We pay our teachers, let us send our children." Not only would they send their children, but they would supervise their education too; and instead of one-eighth of the children more than half would rush to attend. Perhaps you will say that the residents will eventually realize the advantage of education. That would be possible if the youngsters who go to the schools derived obvious benefit from them, but several make such poor use of this benefit that many parents prefer to leave them in ignorance. But suppose that this means were feasible, how should we go about it? We should oblige every landowner to contribute on a yearly basis one-half of one cent per acre in each parish, Catholic or Protestant, without exception. We should make the priest or minister of the more numerous religious denomination, the oldest churchwarden, the oldest captain of militia responsible for receiving this contribution at a stated time, and to place it in the chest of the vestry and use it to pay the teachers, to repair or to help build schools situated no less than two leagues from one another.

Journal de l'Assemblée du Bas-Canada, 1835 - 1836, Appendix 0.o.

48   THE SCHOOLS OF THE FABRIQUES: BISHOP SIGNAY, 1836

Letter from Monseigneur Joseph Signay, Bishop of Quebec, to the priests in the diocese, 2 May 1836.

Sir,

You are no doubt aware that because the act of Legislature which provided for aid to elementary education in the province has been in force only since the first day of the present month, public funds will not be provided for at least this year to support the many schools already established in the parishes of this diocese.

In order to remedy as far as possible the inconveniences which will result from the closing of the majority of these schools, I believe it is my duty to call upon your zeal and invite you to do what is in your power to obtain from your parish at least part of the funds it received under the law which has just expired. To attain this end, I remind you that you can avail yourself of certain Acts (4 George IV, chapter 31 explained by 7 George IV, chapter 20) which authorize *fabriques*[1] in concurrence with the ecclesiastic authority to use one quarter of their annual revenue for the support of one or several of these schools under their direction. Before you then, is the task of making the people of your *fabrique* realize all the benefit which will result from such establishments and of recommending that they do not delay in getting them started. In order to help you out in every possible way in this regard, by this letter I permit your *fabrique* in advance to use one quarter of its revenue for this commendable purpose without requiring further authorization from me.

But since in a great many parishes the revenues from the *fabrique* could be insufficient, I trust you will not neglect to press those who have children to send to school and who thus have an obligation there, to make all the sacrifices their financial means can allow in order to second the efforts of your *fabrique*. I furthermore hope that you will be helped by the influence of those parishioners whose position puts them in a condition to appreciate further the benefits of education.

Finally, Sir, I remain completely confident of your enthusiasm to promptly execute the measure which I have just recommended to you and which I see as very beneficial to the faithful under your care. I am also firmly persuaded that in the present situation you will demonstrate the talents so worthy of praise which have always distinguished the clergy of the country, in furthering education in all social classes.

H. Têtu and C.-O. Gagnon, eds., *Mandements, lettres pastorales et circulaires des évêques de Québec* (Quebec: A. Côte et Cie., 1888), Vol. 3, pp. 341-342.

Note
1. The French word *fabrique* is translated into English as the vestry or vestry board of a parish church.

EDUCATION IN MONTREAL: NEWTON BOSWORTH, 1839   49

Whatever other circumstances are conducive to the prosperity and welfare of a people, there can be no doubt that Education is essential to the perfection and stability of the social state. Intelligence and virtue, founded on religious principle, are the strongest safeguard of individual character, and the best preservative of general utility. That much has been done in different parts of the Province for the advancement of education, it would be improper to deny; but that the system is defective, both in the nature and extent of the instruction it provides, will scarcely admit of a question. The state of education, throughout the Province, it is hoped will undergo a strict and rigorous investigation, and such measures be resorted to as will render its benefits absolutely universal, and counteract the ignorance which is so inimical to good feeling and rational exertion.

In the city of Montreal there appear to be means in existence for imparting instruction, of a slighter or more solid kind, to a great proportion of the young persons resident within it; but it is to be lamented that large numbers of children, especially those of Catholic parents, are suffered to grow up without availing themselves of its benefits. The British population are much more desirous of procuring instruction for their offspring, and hence they are in general more intelligent and enterprising than others. Not that there is a want of capacity among the Canadian youth, for where they have been placed in favourable circumstances they have exhibited abundant proof of the contrary; but the general insensibility of their parents to the value of education, and the almost total absence among them of any rational conception on the subject, render them indifferent to its advantages. Most ardently is it to be desired that means may be discovered to remove this grand obstacle to national improvement. Great numbers of children, however, in both communities, receive instruction in Montreal. In addition to the schools already noticed, there are several respectable academies in the City; as, the Royal Grammar School, in Little St. James Street, conducted by A. Skakel, Esq.; the Rev. Dr. Black's, adjoining St. Paul's Church; Rev. J. Ramsay's, Main Street, St. Lawrence Suburbs; Messrs. Howden & Taggart's, Craig Street; Mr. Workman's in Hospital Street; and Mr. Bruce's in McGill Street. There are also young ladies' schools in high reputation; as Miss Easton's, in Bonaventure Street, Miss Felton's in St. Gabriel Street, and Mrs. Fitzgerald's in Notre Dame Street. The total number of schools, it would be difficult to assign. A few years since, two gentlemen of this city made personal enquiry throughout the place, with a view of determining the point: they found fifty-nine schools of different classes; but it is probable not only that some were overlooked, but that the number is greater now than it was then.

Newton Bosworth, *Hochelaga Depicta; the early history and present state of the City and Island of Montreal* (Montreal: William Greig, 1839), pp. 204–205.

V Politics

In the 1830s, politics in Lower Canada was dominated by issues which had their roots either in the British Conquest of New France in 1760 or in the Constitution of 1791, which created Upper Canada and Lower Canada. Although many issues prominent in the 1830s were variations on old themes, the decade saw the arguments take on a more serious tone. The public mood grew more impatient, more strident, and more uncompromising. By 1837 mutual invective ended in the violence of armed insurrection.

Almost every public issue in Lower Canada in the 1830s was coloured and sharpened by its relationship to the central question of nationalism: how could two widely divergent groups, the English and the French, live amicably in one country? It would be an oversimplification, however, to see the disputes of the 1830s simply in terms of French versus English. As many of the readings illustrate, French-speaking and English-speaking Lower Canadians were divided among themselves over both issues and strategies. Indeed, support for what is usually seen as the French or reform position came from such people as Robert Nelson, John Neilson, Daniel Tracey, and Edmund O'Callaghan.

This section presents documents which not only shed light on important issues, but also show the rising tone of exasperation felt by each side in the face of alleged outrages by the other side.

1. In what ways was the Constitution of 1791 inadequate by the 1830s?
2. What powers did political groups think each branch of government should have? Who was to control finances?
3. What was the nature of society in Lower Canada? Was there to be a place for both French-speaking and English-speaking Lower Canadians?
4. In what ways did the economic situation affect political developments?
5. Did those who supported political change think they could accomplish it peacefully, or did insurrection seem to be the only option left open to them?
6. What British and American ideas or examples influenced the reform movement in Lower Canada?
7. What role did religion and the Roman Catholic Church play in the politics of rebellion?
8. What were the aims and methods adopted by the radicals, the moderates, and the conservatives? What role did French-speaking and English-speaking Lower Canadians play in each of these groups?
9. How widespread was support for the rebellions in Lower Canada?

The first five documents in this section are intended to present a picture of the government of Lower Canada as it was intended to function under the Constitutional Act of 1791, to indicate how it worked in practice, according to contemporary observers, and to present suggestions for reform. The chart in Document 50 illustrates the structure of the colonial government in relation to the government of Britain. Document 51 describes the details of the constitution of the Canadas. In Document 52, Parent presents arguments for changing the role of the Executive Council. In the following reading, the Colonial Secretary, Lord Stanley, instructs the Governor of Lower Canada, Lord Aylmer, on how to react to demands for change and on how the Legislative Council should function. In Document 54, the Assembly of Lower Canada pleads for more power.

PART B: THE POLITICS OF CONFRONTATION

The remaining documents are arranged chronologically and deal with various controversies, the positions taken on these issues by individuals and groups, and the actions and reactions of participants in the disputes. A change in the tone of the debates and a gradual drift away from moderation can be seen as the decade progresses.

Document 55 introduces the policy advocated by the newspaper of the Irish in Lower Canada, the *Vindicator*. It consistently supported the radical cause in the 1830s, urging Papineau and his supporters to emulate the example of Daniel O'Connell, one of Ireland's great orators and agitators of the age. This policy of agitation and confrontation was followed by the radicals right up to the Rebellion in 1837.

Papineau in Document 56 suggests methods by which the government of Lower Canada might be reformed. Instructions from the Colonial Office follow, dealing with the question of who was to control the revenue from crown lands. Newspaper such as the Montreal *Gazette, Le Canadien,* the *Vindicator,* and *La Minerve* played an important role in the political disputes of the 1830s. An article such as "Englishmen! Scotchmen! Irishmen! British Subjects All!" might appear in both the English and the French press, each newspaper printing it for its own reasons and often accompaning it with editorial comment and conclusions.

The feelings of an English-speaking Lower Canadian, H.W. Ryland, are presented in Document 59. His solution foreshadows Lord Durham's solution: unite Upper and Lower Canada in order to assimilate the French. After the "Montreal Massacre" in 1832, which occurred during a bitterly fought by-election in the West Ward of Montreal when British soldiers killed three French Canadians, the tone of the public debate over political power became increasingly bitter. Remarks about the "Montreal Massacre" made two years later by the Colonial Secretary are answered in a bitter reply by Edmund O'Callaghan in the *Vindicator* (Document 60). Later in the same year, O'Callaghan showed his contempt for an appeal to English voters during the 1834 elections, deploring the injection of national prejudices into the campaign (Document 61). O'Callaghan, reacting to a report of 1835 that the control of revenue will be taken away from the Legislative Assembly, advocates preparation for violent resistance.

A description of political parties in Lower Canada, as seen by an English-speaking Lower Canadian, is found in Document 63, along with the writer's suggestion of what should be done. Document 64 presents the program of reforms advocated by the Legislative Assembly, which was dominated by Papineau and his supporters. The most important of the Russell Resolutions are found in Document 65. When news of the Russell Resolutions reached Lower Canada, the radical response was explosive, as shown in the O'Callaghan document, "Agitate! Agitate!! Agitate!!!" A sober warning is given to the radicals by Parent in Document 67. Document 68 from the Montreal *Gazette* is an interesting explanation of the political situation in Lower Canada from an English point of view. Two short excerpts from the *Vindicator* in Document 69 show the path toward violence down which the radicals seemed headed. In Document 70 the Sons of Liberty affirm their dedication to achieve a reformed system of government for Lower Canada. Bishop Signay issues a strong warning to the people concerning their responsibility toward established authority. Parent, deeply disturbed by the actions of the radicals, warns them in Document 71 of the consequences of their actions and calls for moderation on both sides. Document 73 sheds light on the aims of many radicals who followed Papineau and Robert Nelson, the author of the "Declaration of the Provisional Government." The final document is a statistical breakdown of the number of arrests in Lower Canada in 1837 and 1838. It also gives some indication of the type of people who supported the rebellions and what happened to them as a result of their participation in the uprisings.

The Constitution in Theory and Practice

50   BRITISH PARLIAMENTARY GOVERNMENT AFTER THE REFORM BILL OF 1832

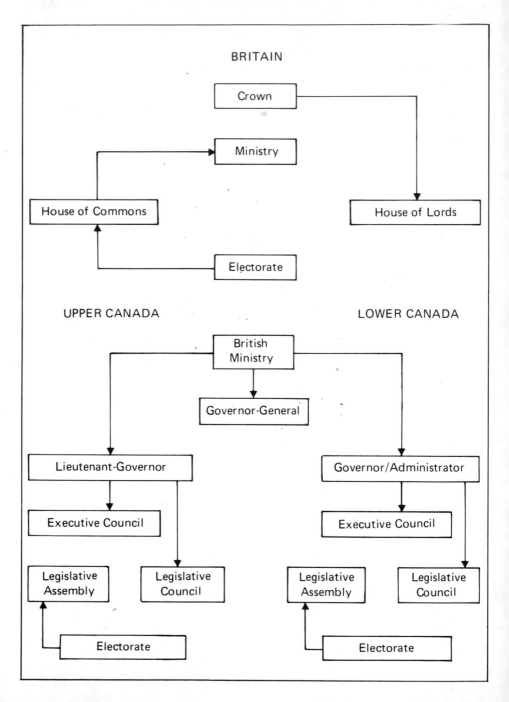

Note
The direction of the arrow indicates the direction in which the appointment or election to office was made. For example, the British Ministry appointed the Governor-General of the Canadas, and the electorate of Upper Canada and Lower Canada elected the Legislative Assembly of Upper Canada and Lower Canada respectively. In the case of the British Ministry, the Prime Minister and his Ministers represented the majority party in the House of Commons and were themselves members of the House of Commons or the House of Lords. Included in the British Ministry was the Colonial Secretary.

According to the Constitutional Act of 1791, the Crown was to appoint a Governor-General with dominion over both Upper and Lower Canada and with nominal control over all of British North America. Under him, each of the Canadas was to have an appointed Lieutenant-Governor. In practice, however, the Governor-General, who resided in Quebec City, handled the office of Lieutenant-Governor or, as he was usually called, Administrator of Lower Canada, while the Lieutenant-Governor of Upper Canada usually acted quite independently of the Governor-General. In reality, then, there was a Governor in Upper Canada and a Governor in Lower Canada.

The members of the Executive Council and the Legislative Council in Upper and Lower Canada were appointed for life by the Governor (Lieutenant-Governor/Administrator) in each colony. Neither the Executive Council nor the Legislative Council was responsible to the Assembly.

The legislative assemblies in Upper Canada and Lower Canada were both elected by those eligible to vote in the colonies. The Legislative Assembly had no control over the Governor, the Executive Council, or the Legislative Council. A measure passed by the Legislative Assembly had to receive the consent of the Legislative Council and the Governor (Lieutenant-Governor/Administrator) before it became law. Even then, the British government could rescind a law any time within two years of its passage.

Throughout the colonial period, the franchise was closely associated with possession of property. It was usual to require a minimum real, rental, or assessed value, although this practice was often neglected in the early years. The franchise in Upper and Lower Canada was fixed by the Constitutional Act of 1791 at a freehold of 40 shillings annual value in rural ridings and ownership or occupancy of a dwelling house and grounds worth £5 or £10 per year in urban ridings. This remained unchanged until 1856, when an assessment franchise was introduced. Other qualifications required that a voter be a male, at least twenty-one years of age, and a British subject.

THE CONSTITUTION AND GOVERNMENT OF LOWER CANADA
51

The authorship of the following reading is not certain; Robert Christie, a member of the House of Assembly, reported that it was supposed to have been written by Sir John Harvey, who later became Lieutenant-Governor of Prince Edward Island (1836), New Brunswick (1837), Newfoundland, and finally, Nova Scotia. Christie was of the opinion, however, that it was written by Lieutenant-General Evans, who served with distinction in Canada.

A MILITARY MAN'S IDEAS ON THE CONSTITUTION AND GOVERNMENT OF LOWER CANADA

The constitution of Canada differs essentially from that of every other colony of Great Britain. It is in fact an epitome of the constitution of England, the only point of difference is, that the seats in the Legislative Council are not like those of the Peers of England, hereditary.

In conducting the Government of this Colony this strict analogy to the constitution of the parent state should never be lost sight of, nor can those general principles of Government, applicable to other colonies, be always safely applied to this.

Let us see how the assertion can be borne out. The jealousy with which the people of *all* colonies view the measures of Government is doubtless quickened in *this* by the circumstances of their being of a different extraction, and professing a religion different from that of their rulers. To this may be added the influence and example of those revolutionary principles which are fast spreading over this continent, and which, though wholly inapplicable to a people enjoying a degree of freedom and happiness unparalleled in the world, must still be reckoned among the causes, not the least powerful, by which the turbulent and the factious mislead the ignorant and the weak. To a people in no respect identified with their rulers, French in their origin, their language, their habits, their sentiments, their religion,— English in nothing but in the glorious constitution which that too liberal country has conferred upon them,—the sole effect of this boon has been to enable them to display, in a *constitutional manner*, those feelings of suspicion, distrust and dislike, by which the conduct of their representatives would warrant us in believing them to be animated towards their benefactors.

The House of Assembly of Lower Canada has not ceased to manifest inveterate hostility to the interests of the Crown, it has withheld its confidence from the local Government, and has, through this blind and illiberal policy, neutralized as far as it could every benefit which that Government has wished to confer upon the people, and that the popular representatives have acted in unison with the feelings of their *constituents* the fact of *their* having invariably sent back those members whose opposition to the Government has been most marked may be thought sufficiently to prove.

Ought not such a people to be left to themselves, to the tender mercies of their gigantic neighbours, whose hewers of wood and drawers of water they would inevitably become in six months after the protection of the British fleets and armies had been withdrawn from them? The possession of this dreary corner of the world is productive of nothing to Great Britain but expense. I repeat that the occupation of Canada is in no respect compensated by any solid advantage.

Nevertheless, it pleases the people of England to keep it much for the same reason that it pleases a mastiff or a bull-dog to keep possession of a bare and marrowless bone towards which he sees the eye of another dog directed. And a fruitful bone of contention it is, and will it prove, betwixt Great Britain and the United States before Canada is merged in one of the divisions of that empire, an event, however, which will not happen until blood and treasure have been profusely lavished in the attempts to defend what is indefensible, and to retain what is not worth having. As we are doomed to retain it, however, let us see how it is to be governed.

[If it] is assumed that the House of Assembly will do as little good and as much mischief as may be in its power, how then are we to promote the former to counteract the latter? Happily, the constitution which ministers what is baneful in the powers which it gives to the Lower House presents us with an antidote in those with which it has clothed the upper one. It is then to the Legislative Council, as to the House of Peers, that we must look for the true constitutional check upon the turbulent demagogues of the Assembly, and if that Council be composed as it ought, the Government of Canada will be carried on with comparative ease and satisfaction, and if the greatest possible quantum of good be not conferred on the people the fault will not rest with the paternal Government of the King or of *his* representative, but with those of the people.

Whatever measures of real utility may originate in the Lower House will meet with no check in the Council, nor will the King's Representative have any hesitation in confirming by his assent that which comes to him recommended by those two branches of the Legislative, and the merit and grace of all such measures will rest, as is just, with those by whom they are originated. On the other hand all measures of a wild, injurious ill-advised party, or impracticable nature, will receive their quietus in the Council, and will not be permitted to reach the Throne. Thus by the interposition of this constitutional check, the most dangerous of all possible collisions (that betwixt the King and the people) is avoided, and the balance of the constitution preserved.

Important as are the duties which the members of the Legislative Council have to perform, it will be obvious that much care should be used in their selection. The weight and importance of this branch of the Legislature, if firmness, moderation and good sense prevail in their Councils, *must* ere long be felt and acknowledged throughout the Province.

With the view to accelerate this state of things, and the advantages to the country, which must flow from it, it is strenuously recommended that every possible degree of publicity be given to its deliberations. The measure of throwing open the Council doors adopted a few years ago, was one step towards this, but it is by no means sufficient. Their proceedings and debates should be published and diffused in the French language throughout the Province.

Their temper, their moderation, their good sense, their genuine patriotism, when contrasted with the opposite qualities, as displayed in the other House, cannot but work their due effect, for let me do the Canadian people the justice to admit, that though they are still *French* (which, having been a British colony upwards of three score years, they ought *not to be* and are *not English*, which for the same reason they ought by this time to have been,) but this is not wholly their fault; they possess many excellent and valuable qualities. They are not loyal as regards the *person* of the King of England, but they are devotedly attached to their country, and I firmly believe prefer the protection of England to that of any other power, *France alone* excepted, and they well know that France *could not* protect them.

Robert Christie, *Interesting Public Documents, and Official Correspondence, Illustrative of, and Supplementary to the History of Lower Canada.* 6 volumes (Montreal: John Lovell, 1848-1855), Vol. VI, pp. 421-424.

REFORM OF THE EXECUTIVE COUNCIL IN LOWER CANADA: *LE CANADIEN,* 1832   52

Le Canadien, November 7, 1832.

. . . There is another branch of our political system about which we have also voiced strong and frequent objections. However, forty years of constitutional government and representations have not yet managed to bring about any reform. The branch is the Executive Council. [This branch possesses] . . . the extraordinary power of doing harm without having to answer for it. Never can we hope for peace and harmony in the government as long as the constitution fails to surround the King's representative with men who are responsible for all administrative acts, and who enjoy the confidence of the Houses, as is the case in every well-organized representative government. The time has come when this colony has become important and prosperous enough to need a regular ministerial organization. . . .

It would thus be desirable to have a body of men, each in a certain department, whose duty it would be to present to the Houses measures dictated by the country's needs; this would not, however, prevent any member from presenting any measure he himself judged suitable. . . . Have a provincial council or ministry composed, as is the case everywhere, of men who are influential in the two Houses. Besides, the political advantage of such an arrangement, you will also have this body of men which, from one end of the year to the other, will be able to see to the perfecting and completion of measures necessary to the country's prosperity and happiness.

To be more convinced of the necessity of a provincial ministry, all one has to do is review the main topics of general interest which have occuped the attention of our Houses for the past few years. . . .

53   THE LEGISLATIVE COUNCIL: LORD STANLEY, 1833

Lord Stanley, British Colonial Secretary, to Lord Aylmer, on 6 June 1833. Lord Aylmer (1775–1850) was Administrator of Lower Canada from 1830 to 1835. He offered seats in the Executive Council to the radicals Papineau and Neilson, but they declined. Papineau held him responsible for the deaths of three French Canadians in a riot in Montreal during the 1832 election.

I have received and laid before His Majesty, George IV, the address of the Legislative Council. His Majesty receives with satisfaction the expression of loyalty and attachment to the Constitution which are contained in this address, and he is readily induced to believe the assurance that the great body of His Canadian Subjects do not participate in the views of those who would be desirous to effect extensive changes in the fundamental institution of the Country; yet His Majesty cannot but wish that in laying at the foot of the Throne the expressions of their own feelings of loyalty and attachment they have abstained from using, with reference to the other branch of Legislature, language less temperate in its tone than is consistent with their own dignity, or calculated to maintain or restore a good understanding between the two bodies. More especially His Majesty laments the introduction of any word which should have the appearance of ascribing to a class of His Subjects of one origin views at variance with the allegiance which they owe to His Majesty. On all classes alike His Majesty relies for a cheerful and willing obedience to the Laws. To all Classes he will ever extend His paternal protection and the Legislative Council may rest assured that He will not fail to secure to all the Constitutional Rights and Liberties which they enjoy by their participation in British Institutions.

I have also laid before the King the Address of the House of Assembly. I cannot pass over this document without observation. The object of this Address is to pray His Majesty to sanction a National Convention of the People of Canada for the purpose of superseding the Legislative Authorities, and taking into their consideration in which of two modes the Constitution of Lower Canada shall be altogether destroyed. Whether by the introduction of the Elective principle or by the entire abolition of the Legislative Council. On the mode proposed His Majesty is willing to put no harsher construction than that of extreme inconsiderateness: to the object sought to be attained His Majesty can never be advised to assent, as deeming it inconsistent with the very existence of Monarchical Institutions. To every measure which may secure the independence and raise the character of the Legislative Council His Majesty will be most ready to assent. In

1828 a Committee of the House of Commons carefully investigated the grievances alleged by the inhabitants of the Canadas, and among them the Constitution of the Legislative Council was a matter of serious deliberation. The Committee reported that one of the most important subjects to which their enquiries had been directed was the state of the Legislative Council in both the Canadas, and the manner in which those Assemblies had answered the purposes for which they were instituted. The Committee strongly recommended that a more independent character should be given to those Bodies, that the majority of their Members should not consist of persons holding offices at the pleasure of the Crown, and that any other measures that might tend to connect more intimately that branch of the Constitution with the interest of the Colonies would be attended with the greatest advantage. With respect to the Judges, with the exception only of the Chief Justice, whose presence on particular occasions might be necessary, the Committee entertained no doubt that they had better not be involved in the political business of the House. An examination of the Constitution of the Body at that period and the present will sufficiently show in what spirit His Majesty's Government have laboured to accomplish the wishes of Parliament. The House of Assembly state correctly that it has often been avowed that the people of Canada should see nothing in the Institutions of neighbouring Countries to which they should look with envy. I have yet to learn that His Majesty's Subjects in Canada entertain such sentiments at present, or that they desire to copy in a Monarchical Government all the Institutions of a Republic, or to have the mockery of an Executive absolutely dependent for its existence upon a popular body usurping the whole authority of the state. I am not prepared to advise His Majesty to recommend to Parliament so serious a step as the repeal of the Act of 1791, whereby the Institutions of this Country were conferred separately upon the Provinces of Upper and Lower Canada; serious as are the difficulties by which Your Lordship's Administration is beset, they are yet not such as to induce me to despair of the practical working of the British Constitution: but should events unhappily force upon Parliament the exercise of its supreme Authority to compose the internal dissenters of the Colonies, it would be my object and my duty as a Servant of the Crown to submit to Parliament such modifications of the Charter of the Canadas as should tend, not to the introduction of Institutions inconsistent with Monarchical Government, but to maintaining and strengthening the connexion with the Mother Country by a close adherence to the spirit of the British Constitution, and by preserving in their proper place, and within their due limits, the mutual rights and privileges of all Classes of His Majesty's Subjects.

Annual Report of the Public Archives of Canada, 1931 (Ottawa, 1932), pp. 297–298.

THE LEGISLATIVE ASSEMBLY, 1836

54

In this extract, the Assembly of Lower Canada petitions the Governor, Lord Gosford, for more power.

The presence in the Province of certain so-called authorities, whose powers and prerogatives can be found neither in the constitution nor in any other law, has so often been cited by Your Excellency and the executive authorities of the Mother Country as something which delays the re-establishment of order and the granting of improvements requested by the people that we cannot prevent ourselves from voicing a few general observations which cannot have escaped any public figure.

We believe that this Assembly is the legitimate organ, authorized by all the classes of inhabitants of the country, and that its representations are the constitutional expression of their wishes and needs. We believe that the impartial exercise we have made of our powers for the protection and happiness of all ought to have inspired a confidence which was merited by our making solemn use of these high privileges. However, it can only be as a result of unjust distrust of this Assembly and of the people of this province that His Majesty's government has rejected our requests in order to abide by a small number of individuals foreign to the country, whose fate was entrused to them and whose vague and subordinate mission cannot have been in keeping with any independent authority recognized by the constitution whose spirit His Majesty wishes above all to retain. It is thus that a force acting out of order and in opposition to order has succeeded in forming connections only with those who adhered to the same follies, and who, long-since declared enemies of this Assembly and people, are taking advantage of the system of double politics which has up to the present time been responsible for the misfortune of the country. . . .

Journaux de la Chambre d'Assemblée Législative du Bas-Canada, Session 1836, 30 September 1836.

The Politics of Confrontation

<table>
<tr><td>CALL TO ACTION—THE IRISH EXAMPLE:
VINDICATOR, 1829</td><td>**55**</td></tr>
</table>

This excerpt from an editorial of 19 May 1829, in the Vindicator, *the newspaper of the Irish in and around Montreal, discusses an allegedly arbitrary decision made by the Lieutenant-Governor of Upper Canada that was upheld by the British government. The editorial goes on to suggest how the people of the Canadas can obtain justice. Daniel O'Connell, referred to in the excerpt, was an Irish political leader of the nineteenth century who was popularly known as the "Liberator."*

It may be demanded of us in what manner can the people obtain that justice of which it is evident they are deprived. . . . Let them imitate the people of Ireland, let them imitate the Catholic Association; let an O'Connell and Sheil rise up among them; let them organize themselves into Constitutional Associations, and put their monies together, a small tax voluntarily imposed upon themselves will turn off many a grievous impost hereafter. Let them do all this within the circumference of the law, as British subjects seeking for redress of grievances. . . . They will have oppression driven from the country, and Sir John Colborne kicked to the other side of the Atlantic.

<table>
<tr><td>SUGGESTIONS FOR REFORMING THE
GOVERNMENT: LOUIS-JOSEPH PAPINEAU, 1830</td><td>**56**</td></tr>
</table>

Letter from Louis-Joseph Papineau to John Neilson, 14 November 1830. Papineau, the radical leader, was born in Montreal in 1786. Educated at the Quebec Seminary, he was first elected to the Legislative Assembly in 1810, becoming Speaker from 1815 to 1822, 1825 to 1826, and 1828 to 1837. As the chief orator for the Patriote party, largely organized by Robert Nelson and Edmund O'Callaghan, he took part in a series of mass meetings in the Richelieu Valley which led to the Rebellion of 1837. In this letter Papineau expresses his views on reform to his friend John Neilson, the journalist and politician. Neilson was also a member of the Assembly and sympathetic to the Patriote cause; but he was against violence and did not take part in the rebellion.

. . . You are disposed to believe that the government can be pushed into the right path and will follow it passably well; I am disposed to believe that it goes from bad to worse.

. . . [I am convinced] that it is essential to the peace and good government of the province that its constitution be amended by suppressing the present Legislative Council and replacing it with an elective Council, in which each county will have a member.

[I am convinced that] the court of justice, badly constituted and not enjoying the least respect or public confidence, could not be reformed in the interest of the citizen while the judges controlled the Council and could not consent to increase their work and responsibility.

[I am convinced that] the ungranted lands ought to be put under such regulations as the Legislature will adopt, and that the Jesuit Estates ought to be put at its disposition to aide the general education of the province, and, finally, that we must not proceed to any other measure until these grievances have been satisfied, and request a prorogation of several months to await the response to the representations made to the King and to Parliament. Your imperturbable stoicism will hardly appreciate these novel proposals. But we will be entering a new session of parliament where we will be able to hear such proposals. My scepticism leaves me absolutely incapable of deciding if this is a bad thing. If it is a good thing, it would give me great pleasure if you would write to me giving your opinion. . . .

Quebec Archives, Papineau Papers XI, pp. 516–517.

57 INSTRUCTIONS ON THE TERRITORIAL REVENUE: COLONIAL OFFICE, 1831

A confidential memorandum from Lord Goderich, British Colonial Secretary, to Lord Aylmer, Administrator of Lower Canada, 21 November 1831.

My despatch of this date will fully explain to your Lordship my views as to the system of management which should be pursued with respect to the Crown Lands; There is however one topick connected with the same subject to which I have thought it right not to allude in a communication which is intended to be laid before the Legislature,—I mean the question which may arise with respect to the right of the Crown to the uncontrolled disposal of the Territorial Revenue.—It appears that in their last Session both branches of the Legislature passed Resolutions to the effect, that the Territorial Revenue should be appropriated in the same manner as the Publick income arising from other sources; and in support of this claim, it has been stated, that Lord Dorchester, during his administration of the Province, made in His Majesty's name a promise, that the right of the Crown to this revenue should be surrendered.

It would be with great regret that I should learn that this claim had again been brought forward, since I cannot disguise from myself, that the necessity of making some permanent financial arrangement puts it in the power of the Assembly to insist, if so disposed, upon a compliance with their demands; while at the same time, I think it of the greatest importance that the right of the Crown to this revenue should be maintained—To prevent the renewal of a question which may be so embarrassing, it will be necessary as much as possible to avoid applying this revenue to purposes likely to excite objections on the part of the Assembly, and it will also be proper to lay before them annually, as you have already been instructed, full accounts of the receipts and expenditure of the income arising under this head.

At the time my dispatch was written, in which, in the event of the Assembly sanctioning the proposed financial arrangement, I instructed you to pay out of the Territorial Revenue the Salaries of the Bishop and Clergy, now paid out of the Army

Extraordinaries, I was not aware that any question as to the right of the Crown to dispose of that revenue was likely to arise. The change of circumstances requires a corresponding change in the course to be pursued, it is therefore the intention of His Majesty's Government to consider some other means of putting an end to the practice of which the impropriety is so manifest: but in the meantime it will be advisable to abstain from paying any portion of these Salaries from the funds in question. Should the financial arrangement adopted by the Assembly be such as to place at the disposal of the Government any surplus from the Territorial revenue, the manner of applying it, which would at once be the most proper in itself and the most likely to give satisfaction to the Province, would be to undertake works of local improvement. That portion of this revenue which arises from the sale of land, ought indeed, strictly speaking, to be invariably thus applied. Land may be considered the capital possessed by the Colony; and the funds obtained by the alienation of that capital, should be invested as income for its permanent benefit, not employed to meet current expenditure. The natural, indeed almost the only wise mode of investment is that presented by undertaking works of local improvement; and it would be highly desirable, that a portion of the Sums derived from the Sale of Land, should as early as possible be so applied.

Such a course would, I hope tend to avert any embarrassing question upon the rights of the Crown, and rendering more generally acceptable that mode of disposing of the waste Lands which, I have already instructed Your Lordship to adopt.

In conclusion I have only to add, that in the hope I entertain that the question respecting the Revenue may not again be agitated, I am encouraged no less by the reliance I place upon Your Lordship's great personal influence, than by my confidence, that the concessions which have been made to the wishes of the inhabitants of Lower Canada will have removed from their minds every feeling of jealousy and discontent.

Annual Report of the Public Archives of Canada, 1931 (Ottawa, 1932), pp. 244–245.

ENGLISHMEN! SCOTCHMEN! IRISHMEN! BRITISH SUBJECTS ALL! *GAZETTE*, 1832   58

This excerpt from an article which appeared first in the Montreal Gazette, *27 November 1832, and three days later in* Le Canadien, *illustrates the increasing stridency and drift toward extremism. It is also an example of a tactic used by those involved in the debates taking place in the 1830s: an article might appear first in an English-language newspaper and shortly after in a French-language newspaper, this time accompanied by editorial comment usually taking issue with the original article or editorial.*

ENGLISHMEN! SCOTCHMEN! IRISHMEN! BRITISH SUBJECTS ALL!—The time has arrived when a temporizing policy as regards the affairs of this Province is disgraceful and dishonourable, not to say criminal. An overweening faction, hostile to BRITISH ascendancy, has openly proclaimed intentions and designs opposed to your interests and is strenuously labouring to rob you of your dearest rights. The lands of CANADA were purchases of FRENCHMEN by our brave countrymen on the battle plains of

ABRAHAM, and your renowed progenitors paid the price with their heart's blood. The conquest and possession achieved by BRITISH valour was confirmed to us by the King of FRANCE, who fully ceded to us by the treaty of PARIS, a country which victory had already made our own. CANADA, therefore, BRITONS, is yours. The lands washed by the ATLANTIC on the east, and by the PACIFIC on the west, as far as the POLAR SEAS, are all yours. They are yours, for colonization, at your own time and pleasure, as it shall suit you to appropriate them for your use and benefit. BRITISH generosity (for when were conquering BRITONS ungenerous) gave to the conquered people the lands they were individually possessed of at the period of the conquest, and secured them undisturbed enjoyment of their property and their religion. History presents no parallel to such clemency, moderation, liberality on the part of the conquerors to the conquered. But the victors conferred a boon far greater. To a most unreasonable demand made by the vanquished in the 41st article of the Capitulation of MONTREAL, the BRITISH conqueror benignly replied, that the inhabitants who shall remain in the country shall become SUBJECTS OF THE KING. . . .

---

59   LOWER CANADIAN POLITICS: H. W. RYLANDS, 1833

A letter from H. W. Rylands to Lord Aylmer, the Administrator of Lower Canada, 14 August 1833. Rylands had come to Canada in 1793 as secretary to the Governor-General, Lord Dorchester. He was Clerk of the Executive Council of Lower Canada from 1793 to 1838, and a member of the Château Clique.

. . . If the preposterous pretensions of the Assembly to proscribe by an annual Bill the terms and conditions on which every servant of the Crown in the Province shall be admitted to office were acceded to, few Englishmen would wish for office here, and emigration to this part of the British dominions would be put an end to till such time as the rapidly increasing population of Upper Canada should pour down upon and overwhelm the French inhabitants of the Lower Province, and this time it appears to me is not far distant for, by all we hear and read concerning the improvements in that of His Majesty's dominions, we are justified in believing that its population is augmented by the adoption of a system which produces as great and astonishing effects as those derived from steam in the various uses to which it is applied.

I feel confident therefore that the policy of Government with respect to the Canadas must shortly be changed, and that their union under one Legislature must soon take place.

I cannot on this occasion refrain from noticing the deplorable state to which the officers of Government in this Province are reduced by the withholding of their salaries for so long a period. The means of counteracting the intentions of the leaders of the Assembly appeared to me so evident, and so much within the power of the Imperial Government, that I entertained no doubt of the success of Your Lordship's endeavours to procure common justice for them. Till this is obtained the political state of Lower Canada will be such as was never before witnessed in a British Colony, and I apprehend that the next Session of the Provincial Legislature will be as unsatisfactory to Your Lordship as it will be to every man who is influenced by principles of loyalty, and a sincere attachment to the British constitution.

Robert Christie, *Interesting Public Documents and Official Correspondence, History of Lower Canada*, Vol. VI (Montreal, 1855), pp. 434–435.

REACTION TO THE MONTREAL MASSACRE OF 1832: EDMUND O'CALLAGHAN, 1834   **60**

In the 1832 by-election for the West Ward of Montreal, Dr. Daniel Tracey, the founder of the Vindicator *in 1828, ran for election. After a very close election in which each side charged the other with intimidation and corrupt practices, Tracey was elected. An English-speaking candidate acceptable to both English and French voters was tradi-tionally chosen to balance the French-speaking member from the East Ward of Montreal, but Tracey, though not French, was not acceptable to the English voters. The most serious aspect of the election, however, was the riot that took place on 21 March 1832. British troops were called out. Three French Canadians were killed. The incident, which came to be called the "Montreal Massacre," embittered many people against British rule.*

Edmund O'Callaghan (1797–1880), doctor, politician, journalist, historian, and archivist, was born in Ireland and came to Canada in 1823. He wrote this editorial in the Vindicator, *of which he was editor, on 6 June 1834. Later elected representative for Yamaska in 1834, he became one of the organizers of the Rebellion of 1837 and was present at the uprising of St. Denis on November 23 of that year. He fled to the United States and did not return to Lower Canada.*

The sneering manner in which Mr. Stanley [in a speech] refers to the "massacre" of 21st May [1832], will not we hope escape the notice of the people. It was "nothing more than an election disturbance, in which two or three persons were killed." A mere moonshine affair, unworthy of the least consideration.

From one who has been accustomed to scenes of blood in Ireland, where peelers, and red coats think nothing of shooting the people, much commiseration was not to be expected. The Right Honourable Secretary is, however, egregiously mistaken if he imagines that AMERICANS will permit themselves or their brethren to be shot with the same *sang froid* that "*mere* Irish" are periodically dispatched. . . . The Massacre of the Citizens of Boston was succeeded five years afterwards, by the battle of Lexington —(fifteen months later) by the Declaration of Independence. . . . We warn the people to be on their guard. A deep laid, widespread conspiracy is on foot against them. Those confided with authority in the province and the gang of bum-bureaucrats who reside both here and in England, have coalesced and with Stanley at their head, their object is the enslaving of the permanent inhabitants of the country in the hope of ultimately ruling the land. . . . It is yet time. See ye to your liberties and be not SLAVES.

61   MONTREAL ELECTION APPEAL: *VINDICATOR*, 1834

In response to a charge that the Lower Canadian reformers were appealing only to French Canadians in the November election of 1834, O'Callaghan charges that it is the English party that is fostering national distinctions. The following excerpt from the Vindicator *of 5 November 1834 refers to a speech made by a Mr. Collard, one of the English party and a partisan of one of the Tory candidates in the election, a Mr. Stuart. Papineau and his followers won a sweeping victory in the election of 1834.*

He [Mr. Collard] would call upon the sons of old England, the descendents of those proud nobles and bold yeomen who signed the great Charter. Forward to the Poll! T'is the voice of your country calls you. Children of the mist and the mountain, sons of the land and field and flood, of the free kilt and waving plume—Scotchmen! Forward! T'is a Stuart calls. Last, though not least, lads of Old Erin! To the Poll! Onward in the cause of the rose and the shamrock! . . .

Ah! now we have the saddle on the right horse. We thought we would come to it at last! and a more vulgar, common-place bombastic appeal to national prejudices, of the most common kind, we never witnessed. . . .

62   MOVE TOWARD VIOLENCE: *VINDICATOR*, 1835

The following excerpt is taken from an article in the Vindicator *of 4 August 1835, in which O'Callaghan replies to a report in the Quebec* Gazette *on the possibility that revenue will be removed from the control of the Legislative Assembly.*

Each honest man in Canada, should, *if such a measure be attempted, keep his rifle in order and his powder dry.* . . . The contingency to which our Correspondent alluded was, the removal of the Revenues of the Colony from the control of the House of Assembly. . . .

So far from shrinking from a participation of the opinions above stated, we hesitate not to say that there is not an honest man in the Province but would feel himself called on to act up to its letter, should an attempt be made to remove the public Revenue from the control of the Assembly. The people of this Province are not reduced to such a state of mental slavery altogether, as to suffer, whilst they have rifle and powder-flask, so outrageous a violation to be committed on their rights as British subjects.

POLITICAL PARTIES IN LOWER CANADA: T. FRED ELLIOTT, 1835 — 63

This is an excerpt from a private letter dated 24 October 1835, written by T. Fred Elliott, the Secretary to the Gosford Commission, to his friend Henry Taylor, at the Colonial Office in London. Lord Gosford, who became Governor of Lower Canada in 1835, was to head a commission that would advise the British government on a course of action for Lower Canada.

Dear Taylor,

Although I have abstained until now from talking politics in the letters I have written you, I should not like you to be completely unaware of the nature of the scene in which we are playing a role, and today, the day before the reunion of the Assembly, I want to draw you as good a picture of Canadian society as I can at the present time. Whether the picture is exact or not, at least it was not taken from a single source or taken ready-made; it is the result of very general and careful research.

In England we are accustomed to seeing only two parties in Canada: the English and the French. But the fact is that there are three—the Official party, the English party and the French party) aside from important French classes which are completely distinct from the party known by the latter name.

(The official party—or, as the French call it, the bureaucratic party—is composed of a small number of elderly men who hold the highest positions. These men seem eager for privileges, jealous of their authority, and ready to take offence at any examination of allegations on the part of the people. Most of them are dull, and those who are not are said to be mercenary. What they are is of little importance. Whatever influence they might have exerted in the past with the cooperation of weak governors, today, they are devoid of all real power, since they have neither relations in England nor influence in the province) . . .

Very much different from this weak body is the real ''English party.'' The latter is composed of almost all the merchants to whom are added big landowners, and a group of the youngest and most intelligent civil servants. This party possesses a lot of intelligence, substantial resources and even more credit) Moreover, it has that mutual confidence, precision and unity of purpose which our compatriots—we have to do them this justice—know better than any other people how to give to political associations. Moreover, this imposing body enjoys a great advantage at the moment, because of the moderate tone it is able to take in contrast to the violence of its adversaries: this earns it the good-will, if not the open support, of that large part of society which prefers security and a quiet life to all other things (And yet, I do not like the English party. It has all the ambition to dominate that the French party has; and, in my opinion, it is ready to employ less scrupulous means to gain its ends.)

'The French party,' if we limit this name to those who have their own ideas, plans and sentiments, seems to be just about synonymous with the majority in the General Assembly, or rather, with the small portion of this majority which has some idea of politics. In imitation of what has always been, the Assembly is composed principally of lawyers, doctors and farmers. The latter are very ignorant of politics and politics are immaterial to them; they aspire to their commissions only, as they say, on account of the profit they derive. During a long session, the salary of $2.00 a day allows them to save considerable amounts, particularly in view of the fact that their wives are usually capable of directing the farmwork in their absence. Just as you have heard, it is true that two or three deputies do not know how to write their names, and it is said that others, who had the wit to learn to draw the letters which make up their signatures, cannot penetrate the mysteries of reading and writing. Without going into too much detail, I can tell you once and for all, that the bulk of the Assembly is inert, and that the few deputies gifted with activity and intelligence act in total submission to Papineau, who inspires in them a profound respect. . . .

. . . Indeed, the real question between the parties in this country is a question of time. In the bottom of their hearts, the French cannot be unaware that they are enjoying a lot of power at the moment; but they see that this power is continually tending to pass into other hands and this is what makes them uneasy and jealous. On the other hand, the English must feel sure that the domination of the country will eventually be concentrated in their race; but they are impatient and want to seize the privilege before they have legitimately secured it. Today the two sides are in their right place. However, each of them is striving, the one to precipitate, the other to avoid, a transition which will ultimately be the specific result of the province's institutions.

. . . Here is, then, the résumé of my credo;—To win over the French Canadians and educate them in the art of governing is the safest and most appropriate policy for the present and also the policy which will most lead to substantial and lasting advantages in the future; but the attempt will probably be thwarted by the perversity and egotism of various sides.

Annual Report of the Archives of Canada, 1883 (Ottawa, 1884).

64 RESOLUTIONS OF THE ASSEMBLY OF LOWER CANADA, 1836

Resolved, That it is the opinion of this committee, that the political reforms which this House and the good people of this Province have been for a great many years endeavouring to obtain, have at various epochs been explained by the votes, resolutions and addresses of this House, and by the petitions of the people themselves. That the principal object of those reforms:—To render the Executive Council of this Province directly responsible to the representatives of the people, in conformity with the principles and practice of the British Constitution as they obtain in the United Kingdom; to extend the principle of election to the Legislative Council, which branch of the Provincial Legislature has hitherto proved, by reason of its independence of the people, and of its imperfect and vicious constitution insufficient to perform the functions for which it was originally designed; to place under the constitutional and salutary control of this House the whole of the revenues levied in this Province from whatever source arising; to abolish pluralities, or the cumulation in one person of several or incompatible offices; to procure the repeal of certain statutes passed by the Imperial Parliament, in which the people of this Province are not and cannot be represented, which acts are an infringement of the rights and privileges of the Legislature of this colony, and are injurious to the interests of the people thereof; to obtain over the internal affairs of this Province, and over the management and settlement of the wild lands thereof (for the advantage and benefit of all classes of His Majesty's subjects therein without distinction), that wholesome and necessary control which springs from the principles of the Constitution itself, and of right belongs to the Legislature, and more particularly to this House as the representatives of the people; which reforms are specially calculated to promote the happiness of His Majesty's subjects in this Province; to draw more close the ties which attach the colony to the British empire, and can in no way prejudice or injure the interests of any of the sister Provinces.

W. P. M. Kennedy, *Documents of the Canadian Constitution, 1759–1915* (Toronto: Oxford University Press, 1918), p. 426.

THE RUSSELL RESOLUTIONS, MARCH 1837

65

Lord John Russell, British Colonial Secretary, introduced new resolutions into the House of Commons on 2 March 1837. The Russell Resolutions, as they were called, represented a shift in the policy of the British government toward Lower Canada from one of conciliation, as represented by Lord Gosford's commission, to one of firmness. The new policy refused any new concessions to the Legislative Assembly and allowed the Governor to use funds from the provincial treasury even if the Assembly had refused to vote them. On receiving the news of the Russell Resolutions, the radicals mounted an even stronger campaign of agitation and organization.

4. That in the existing state of Lower Canada, it is unadvisable to make the Legislative Council of that province an elective body; but that it is expedient that measures be adopted for securing to that branch of the Legislature a greater degree of public confidence.

5. That while it is expedient to improve the composition of the Executive Council in Lower Canada, it is unadvisable to subject it to the responsibility demanded by the House of Assembly of that province.

6. That the legal title of the North American Land Company to the land holden by the said Company, by virtue of a grant from his Majesty, under the public seal of the said province, and to the privileges conferred on the said company by the Act for that purpose made, in the fourth year of his Majesty's reign, ought to be maintained inviolate.

7. That it is expedient, that so soon as provisions shall have been made by law, to be passed by the Legislature of the said province of Lower Canada, for the discharge of lands therein from feudal dues and services, and for removing any doubts as to the incidents of the tenure of land in fee and common soccage in the said province, a certain Act made and passed in the sixth year of the reign of his late Majesty King George IV, commonly called "The Canada Tenures Act," and so much of another Act passed in the third year of his said late Majesty's reign, commonly called "The Canada Trade Act," as relates to the tenures of land in the said province, should be repealed, saving nevertheless to all persons all rights in them vested under or by virtue of the said recited Acts.

8. That for defraying the arrears due on account of the established and customary charges of the administration of justice, and of the civil government of the said province, it is expedient, that after applying for that purpose such balance as shall, on the said 10th day of April, 1837, be in the hands of the Receiver-General of the said province, arising from his Majesty's hereditary, territorial, and casual revenue, the Governor of the said province be empowered to issue from and out of any other part of his Majesty's revenues, in the hands of the Receiver-General of the said province, such further sums as shall be necessary to effect the payment of the before-mentioned sum of £142,160. 14s. 6d.

9. That it is expedient that his Majesty be authorized to place at the disposal of the Legislature of the said province, the net proceeds of his Majesty's hereditary, territorial, and casual revenue arising within the same, in case the said Legislature shall see fit to grant to his Majesty a civil list for defraying the necessary charges of the administration of justice, and for the maintenance and unavoidable expenses of certain of the principal officers of the civil government of the said provinces.

10. That great inconvenience had been sustained by his Majesty's subjects inhabiting the provinces of Lower Canada and Upper Canada, from the want of some adequate means for regulating and adjusting questions respecting the trade and commerce of the said provinces, and divers other questions, wherein the said provinces have a common interest; and it is expedient that the Legislature of the said provinces respectively be authorized to make provision for the joint regulation and adjustment of such their common interest.

W. P. M. Kennedy, *Documents of the Canadian Constitution, 1759-1915* (Toronto: Oxford University Press, 1918), pp. 435-436.

---

66   AGITATE! AGITATE!! AGITATE!!!
VINDICATOR, APRIL 1837

The Russell Resolutions were greeted with indignation by many of those urging the British government for political reforms in Lower Canada. O'Callaghan, in this article from the Vindicator *of 21 April 1837, again points to the Irish experience and openly calls on the people to agitate for their rights. Lord John Russell and Lord Gosford, the present Colonial Secretary and Governor of Lower Canada respectively, and Lord Dalhousie, a former Governor of Lower Canada, are singled out for their actions.*

HURRAH FOR AGITATION

The O'Connell Cry

It gives us great pleasure to announce, that the feeling created throughout this wealthy and populous district, by Lord John Russell's infamous resolutions, is one of unmixed INDIGNATION. They are met everywhere with "curses not loud but deep" and a fixed, stubborn determination, to resist any and every attempt to enslave the country.

The Reformers are already on the alert. Some preliminary meetings have, we understand, been held, preparatory to calling a meeting of the rich and independent county of *Richelieu*. To the Freeholders of the county in which the Honble. Mr. Debartzeh resides, will belong the honour of being the first to denounce the Honourable renegade and the machiavellian of the treacherous government.

A movement in such a quarter is ominous for the treacherous administration of Lord GOSFORD. It will, we have no doubt, be followed throughout the Province by similar meetings, and before the summer will have gone over their heads, the people of Lower Canada will tell both their Representatives and their rulers, that they are not the stuff from which slaves are made.

It could not be otherwise. Those who have combatted, and successfully combatted, the attempts of DALHOUSIE to pay away their money without the authority of law; those who have, year after year, protested against the unconstitutional interference of the British Parliament in our internal affairs, will not now allow it to go abroad to the world that their principles and protests are nothing better than waste paper. They will not permit it to be said that, at the beck of even a House of Commons, they now sanction what they have up to this day so doggedly, so repeatedly, so consistently, and so honourably resisted.

A combined and dishonourable junction of Whigs and Tories, in a House of Commons "reformed" but in name, may pass Resolutions to annihilate the last remnant of Liberty left to Colonial Legislatures. A House of Lords, the fundamental principle of whose Constitution is inimical to human freedom, may endorse the determination of the combined enemies of freedom in the Lower House, but neither the Resolutions, their authors, nor their supporters, can change the nature of things. Robbery will still be robbery. . . .

Our rights must not be violated with impunity. A howl of indignation must be raised from one extremity of the Province to the other against the ROBBERS, and against all those who partake of the plunder.

HENCEFORTH, THERE MUST BE NO PEACE IN THE PROVINCE, no quarter for the plunderers. Agitate! *Agitate!!* AGITATE!!! Destroy the Revenue; denounce the oppressors. Everything is lawful when our fundamental liberties are in danger. "The guards die; never surrender."

CRITICISM OF THE ACTIONS OF THE PATRIOTES: ETIENNE PARENT, MAY 1837   67

Le Canadien, May 15, 1837.
We cannot support the Patriotes when they say that "the extent of our submission should

henceforth be equal only to the extent of our numbers combined with the sympathies we find elsewhere,'' and further down that ''an unhappy experience obliges us to acknowledge that on the other side of the 45th parallel are our friends and natural allies.'' Have they seriously considered that in these few lines there is a declaration of war in every form against England, and moreover an unequivocal appeal to the neighbouring States, ''our natural allies,'' to overrun our frontiers? Have they seriously considered at the same time that we necessarily find ourselves admitting our weakness and the impossibility of winning our independence in our present position for a long time to come? And have they not sensed the extreme imprudence there was in putting us in a decidedly hostile position vis-à-vis England when the most distant political horizon offers us no solid hope of making ourselves respected in this position? They seem to be making a great deal of ''the sympathies we find elsewhere.'' Alas! We fear greatly that declarations which are so far removed from reality tend to stifle all seeds of sympathy abroad rather than favour their development. . . .

We ask the assemblies which will probably hold session in other counties . . . not to make any declaration which does not carry the seal of wisdom as well as of energetic dignity.

<hr>

68 THE SITUATION IN LOWER CANADA: *GAZETTE*, JULY 1837

Montreal *Gazette*, July 13, 1837.

We had occasion to administer a slight rebuke to the *New York Daily Express* for presuming to intermeddle with the internal affairs of this Province; and, particularly for the insolent and bullying style in which the paper ventured to impose the sympathies of the UNITED STATES in the domestic feuds of a foreign country. . . .

. . . We shall, therefore, in this place, state a few plain facts which, we hope, may have the effect of deterring the *Express*, and all others similarly disposed, from again interesting themselves in our private affairs, or of contributing to the aggrandizement of the one party or the other, while our personal differences remain undecided.

That serious dissensions prevail in the Province, no one will deny; but they are not of such a nature as to excite either the cupidity or the alarm of our Republican neighbours, or to disturb the confidence of the loyal and Constitutional part of the community in their own power to appease and adjust them. These dissensions have their source in the rabid ambition of a vain, but weak party to become independent of the Mother Country, and to establish in this Province an isolated democracy, which would have no connection whatever with ENGLAND and the UNITED STATES. This party dislikes . . . Great Britain because the laws and institution of that country, how much soever they may be extolled in the abstract, are totally adverse, and must be ultimately ruinous to feudal tyranny and democratic despotism. They abjure a connection with the United States, however much they pretend to admire the institutions of that great country, because they are well aware, that the instant they should give in their adhesion to, and throw themselves into the arms of, the Union, their pretended nationality, in respect of habits, manners, language, laws, and religion, would be absorbed by those of the Union—more favourable, in every respect, to freedom, enterprise, and prosperity. This insignificant party, must, therefore, have a little and insignificant nation of their own; and nothing can more clearly demonstrate the ridiculous notions which they entertain upon this subject, than the headlong fury with which they urge and pursue their eager course towards the object in view. But we know they are masters of no craft whatever. In a moral and physical point of view, they are despicable. As politicians, they are actuated by no principles whatever, except personal ambition and aggrandizement—without a particle of real patriotism, magnanimity, or public spirit. As a party, they are zealous and enthusiastic, but cowardly. They are devoid of mutual confidence in each other; and the slightest blow of adversity, would scatter them asunder on the four winds of heaven. As to the "sinews of war," they are wholly destitute of means. As to personal character, they are equally without interest, influence and authority. If they took the field tomorrow, we venture to predict that there are not five hundred sane individuals in CANADA who would be so fool-hardy as to follow them, and thus put all that is dear to them in the world upon a cast.

CALL TO ARMED RESISTANCE: *VINDICATOR*, OCTOBER 1837   **69**

After repeatedly urging the supporters of reform to agitate for change, O'Callaghan, in the following short excerpts from the 3 October and 6 October issues of the Vindicator, *calls for armed resistance against established authority.*

. . . Toryism is the same in Canada as in Ireland. . . . While the vile faction and their vile organs the *Gazette* and *Patriot* threaten the people with clubs, LET THE PEOPLE BE PREPARED TO DEFEND THEMSELVES WITH RIFLES. . . .

. . . *I cannot repeat too often*;—CANADA MUST RELY UPON HER OWN RIGHT ARM FOR JUSTICE.

ADDRESS BY THE SONS OF LIBERTY OF MONTREAL TO THE YOUNG PEOPLE OF THE NORTH AMERICAN COLONIES, OCTOBER 1837   **70**

A statement by the Sons of Liberty, made public on 4 October 1837, in Montreal. The Sons of Liberty was a secret association of young French Canadians formed in 1837 by Louis-Joseph Papineau. The association proclaimed the power of democracy and was formed along military lines.

. . . We maintain that governments are instituted for the advantage of, and can justly exist only with the consent of those governed, and that even if some artificial change should befall human affairs, a government by choice is no less an inherent right of the people. . . . All governments are instituted for the advantage of all the people, not for the honour or profit of a single individual; any claim to govern according to a divine or absolute authority, made by or for any man or any class of men, is blasphemous and absurd. The authority of a mother-country over a colony can only exist as long as it pleases the inhabitants of that colony. Having been settled and populated by these settlers, this country rightfully belongs to them. Consequently, it can be separated from any foreign connection any time that the disadvantages resulting from the fact that the executive power, which is situated far-off, ceases to be in harmony with the local legislature and makes such steps necessary to its inhabitants, in order to protect their lives and liberty or to achieve prosperity. . . .

. . . After seventy-seven years of English domination, we are inclined to regard our country as being in a state of poverty compared to the flourishing republics which had the wisdom to throw off the yoke of monarchy. . . . This so-called protection has paralyzed all our energy. It has conserved all that was defective in our former institutions, thrown the present state of society into confusion, thwarted the free operation of what was good, and opposed any measure of reform or improvement. . . .

. . . Our lands have been sold or given away in defiance of our remonstrances to a company of speculators living on the other side of the Atlantic, or divided among parasitic officials who, for their own interests, combined to form a faction to support a corrupt government, the enemy of the rights and wishes of the people. At the same time, our fathers, relatives and fellow-settlers received only refusals or are unable to obtain these lands, which are lying fallow. . . .

. . . Commercial regulations for this colony, which were adopted in a foreign Parliament are presently in force without our consent. Because of this we find ourselves limited to certain outlets and deprived of the means to extend our trade to all ports of the world, even though Great Britain's markets are not as advantageous to the distribution of our products; from this derives the impotence and inertia of our commercial enterprises.

The country's representation has become a notorious object of mockery. A corrupt executive has constantly worked towards making our Legislative Assembly an instrument for inflicting slavery upon its constituents; and seeing that it was not succeeding in its infamous plan, it made the Assembly's action ineffectual by prorogations or frequent dissolutions or by refusing to sanction laws essential to the people which had been passed unanimously by its representatives.

A legislative council whose members are nominated by an authority which is uninformed about the provinces' affairs, which resides 3,000 miles away and which is composed to a great extent of people who have no sympathy for the country, still exists at present as an ineffectual screen between those who govern and those who are governed, always ready to nullify any attempt at useful legislation. An executive council named in the same way . . . protects pluralism and all the abuses which go with each public department. A governor who is as ignorant as his predecessors and who, following each of their examples, has made himself an official partisan, runs the government machine to the advantage of the minority, caring little for the interests of the majority, or else even determined to place obstacles in its path.

Our grievances have been faithfully and on many occasions submitted to the King and Parliament of the United Kingdom, in resolutions passed by primary assemblies and by our representatives assembled in Parliament, in the humble petitions of the whole nation. We have voiced our remonstrances. . . . No remedy has been effected and, in the end, when the tyranny of those vested with power in the province has reached unbearable limits through the impunity assured them, an ungrateful mother-country is taking advantage of a time of general peace to force us to close our eyes and approve our degradation by threatening us with the violent seizure of our public revenues in defiance of the natural laws and of all principles of law, politics and justice.

Since the present state of degradation of our country is the result of three-quarters of a century of warm devotion to our connection with England and of betrayed confidence in British honour, it would be proving ourselves criminal and born for servitude to limit our resistance to simple representations. . . . A separation between parties has begun: it will never again be possible to reunite them, and this partition will continue with growing force until one of these unforeseen and unexpected events which happens now and then in the course of present times, has furnished us with a favourable opportunity of taking our place among the independent dominions of America. . . .

In consequence, we, the officers and members of the committee of the association of the Sons of Liberty in Montreal, give our solemn promise to our mistreated homeland to each of you, to devote all our energy and to keep ourselves ready to act should circumstances dictate it, in order to procure for this province a reformed system of government, based on the principle of election; a responsible executive government; control by the representative branch of the Legislature of all public revenue from any source whatsoever; the revocation of all laws and charters passed by foreign authority which could infringe upon the rights of the people and its representatives and particularly those which relate to property and tenure of land belonging, be it to the public or to individuals; an improved system for the sale of public lands so that those wishing to settle on them may be able to do so with as little expense as possible; the abolition of pluralism and of the irresponsibility of public officers, and strict equality before the law for all classes regardless of origin, language or religion.

L.-J. Amédée Papineau, *Journal d'un Fils de la liberté réfugie aux Etats-Unis par suite de l'insurrection Canadienne en 1837.* 6 volumes.

CALL FOR MODERATION: ETIENNE PARENT, OCTOBER AND DECEMBER 1837   71

Etienne Parent, who had advocated reform in Lower Canada throughout the 1830s, split from Papineau and his supporters as they moved closer to rebellion. In the first excerpt from Le Canadien *on 9 October 1837, Parent responds to the Address by the Sons of Liberty of Montreal (see the preceding Document). In the second excerpt from* Le Canadien *on 1 December 1837, after hostilities had already broken out, Parent urges moderation.*

Le Canadien, October 9, 1837.
If we are to believe the Montreal papers, our affairs are soon going to be in a state which will simplify them a great deal, for the country's residents will have to choose between peace and civil war, between the King and M. Papineau, between the United States and England. The Sons of Liberty, to the knowledge of their fathers no doubt, have just publicly released a Declaration of Independence, to be acted upon at the first opportu-

nity. The central committee of Deux Montagnes is going to establish tribunals of justice and activate the militia, and we should expect the convention of the Cinq Comtes which is to open on the twenty-third at Village Papineau, St. Charles, not to be far behind. Now there is a whole government there. It remains to be seen if the present government will hand over its resignation to the new one peacefully. If this whole thing is not a ridiculous farce, it will certainly be a terrible tragedy, which is going to begin, as soon as possible, and in the meantime, we will say that if there is any wisdom and patriotism in the conduct of the Montreal agitators, if in this conduct there is anything but lunacy and disastrous delusions, we give up calculating the course of political events in this country forever.

Le Canadien, December 1, 1837.
We state and we will repeat that a solemn and universal declaration on the part of the rest of the population will open the people's eyes to that deluded, deceived group of radicals who are rushing forward and throwing themselves into the abyss. They will drag along all of us with them if all those who have not been possessed by madness do not hasten to ward off the storm. This is not the blood of our friends and brothers we are speaking about, the ruin of our land, the burning of our towns, the ruin and misery of the people which will be the immediate consequence of the pursuit of such a foolish undertaking. These are terrible things it is true, but these are not irreparable. Time heals all wounds. We are speaking to you about an even worse evil because this evil is irreparable. We speak about the loss for an indefinite period of our political, civil and religious rights which we now possess; . . . The Montreal *Gazette* . . . speaks of nothing less than stripping *Canadiens* of all their political rights, all the advantages *Canadiens* enjoy under the government. In a word, the [*Gazette*] would make us slaves. . . .

---

72   BISHOP SIGNAY'S *MANDEMENT*, DECEMBER 1837

Bishop Signay became Bishop of Quebec in 1833. During his incumbency he dealt with problems arising from cholera outbreaks and the rebellions of 1837 and 1838. This is the mandement *he issued on 11 December 1837, ordering public prayers at the time of the rebellion.* Mandements *were addressed to the priests and parishioners in a diocese. They were more than just pastoral letters, in that they usually instructed the faithful about their duties as Roman Catholics in specific circumstances.*

Greetings and blessings from Our Lord to the clergy and faithful of this diocese.

Circumstances oblige us to raise our voice to remind the faithful committed to our care about their duty in relation to the present government, and to inform them what is happening in the Montreal area which is today the worst subject afflicting the residents of this province.

You know that some who are blinded by mistaken patriotism have endeavoured to have views favouring insubordination prevail in Lower Canada. These distressing doctrines have produced their results. A considerable number of our fellow citizens who have adopted them without foreseeing the deplorable results have already become the victims of their too confident credulity.

However painful it is to our heart to place in front of your eyes facts which will grieve you, we cannot, nevertheless, exempt ourselves from this. These facts provide the occasion to caution you against the evil doctrines which brought this situation about.

There is no doubt, Dearly Beloved Brethren, and we feel a real consolation in recognizing it, that these beliefs are held by only a small number of people in this diocese and that the majority of the people have always shown loyalty and fidelity to the government. But this small number of people are part of the flock that divine Providence has charged us with instructing. We must make an accounting to the shepherd of all souls. We would be neglecting our essential duty not to do what we can in order to disabuse and reclaim from their error those who depend on us.

It is not necessary here to enter into a detailed account of the authorities on which the obedience that all the faithful owe to the established authority is based. The principles of our sacred religion are so clear and so precise that absolutely no Catholic who wishes to remain a Catholic can call them into question. What is sufficient for you to know is that the Church, led by the Holy Spirit, and stressing the lessons of Our Shepherd, Jesus Christ, and his apostles, has never ceased to teach its children that they must render unto Caesar that which is Caesar's (Mark, XII: 17), that everyone must submit to the superior civil power which governs them (Romans, XIII), and that this should be done not because of fear of the outcome of rebellion but because of an indispensible duty (Romans, XIII: 5). To oppose the established power is to oppose God and to expose oneself to the weight of God's vengeance.

Following such formal declarations from the Scriptures to which we could add the testimony of our Fathers in the Church. It is being said that your shepherds, in recommending that you submit to the authorities, are straying from their duty and that they are intervening in political issues which are not in their jurisdiction. Nonetheless it is time in the eyes of all good Catholics that priests have only to teach truth all the time, a truth that is one of the foundations of Christian morality, a truth that they can say nothing of to their flock without betraying their trust.

We do not question the right of people to look for legal and constitutional ways of remedying abuses about which they believe they are right to complain. However, to have recourse to insurrection to achieve this goal is to use a method that we say is not only ineffective, imprudent, and disastrous for those using it, but also sinful in the eyes of God and our holy religion. It is to throw oneself into an abyss of irreparable evil under the pretext of avoiding evil. The experience of all the centuries teaches that man advances nothing on earth except by conforming to the ultimate truth.

In fact, if man studies history, he will find practically no revolution which was not the cause of great disasters: blood flowing freely; families plunged into mourning or reduced to misery by the violent death of their breadwinner; property devastated or stolen from the real owner. This is only a small picture of the woe begotten by revolutions. We deeply regret that some of these woes have befallen one of the most flourishing parts of the country.

Thus, Dearly Beloved, when we strive to convince you of the obligation to submit to authority that the Gospel imposes on all of us, we do not intend only to bring home to you the reality of a duty imposed by religion. We also want to spare you the distressing harm we have just outlined to you. In addition, we want to insure your happiness and that of your family and your society.

On this point, do your priests not deserve to be heard? Will they be the only people who are not free to open their mouths to enlighten you on the subject of your real interests? Can you believe that in urging you to loyal obedience, their intent is to compromise themselves? No, Dearly Beloved Brethren. Their constant effort and their generous sacrifices to help further the prosperity of our country do not allow such a damaging suspicion to be formed. Their conduct at all times is unequivocal proof of the affection they have for their fellow citizens. This assures them an undeniable right to your confidence.

We thus hope that you will lend an attentive ear to our exhortations and to those of those worthy people in the holy ministry who co-operate with us. We hope that you are considering more seriously thanever all the consequences that civil war would involve for our dear country. We also hope that, without renouncing your political privileges, you will apply yourselves to demonstrate by your actions and your words that you are filled with the loyalty to Great Britain that your forefathers left you as a heritage and that they proved on more than one occasion even at the cost of their lives.

But it is not enough, Dearly Beloved Brethren, that we bid you to maintain your vigil against anything which could disturb the peace you have enjoyed until now. We must also urge you to raise your hands toward Heaven in supplication, to beg of our Merciful Father that He may preserve this blessed peace among you, and restore it in that part of the Province where it has unfortunately been disturbed.

Wherefore, in the Holy Name of God, we do set down and ordain, the following:

1. A solemn mass will be celebrated in all parishes of our diocese, the first day on which it will be convenient after the publication of the present pastoral letter. This mass will be consistent with the office of the day; the Pro quacumque necessitate prayer will be added to it, and it will be followed by the prayers prescribed herafter.

2. Those parish priests charged with serving two parishes will celebrate this mass in one or the other, at their convenience.

3. Every Sunday and every holy day of obligation, in all churches and chapels in our diocese where mass is celebrated publicly, the priest who performs the mass, be it in the parish, in the convent, or a solemn high mass, will not thereafter leave the steps of the altar until he has recited, aloud and on bended knee, with the people responding, either the Lord's Prayer five times and five Hail Mary's or the Litanies of the Blessed Virgin. We hope that those among the faithful who will be unable to attend holy service on those days will say the same prayer with their families.

4. Every priest will add the aforementioned prayer to the mass, except to masses of first class holy days, the solemn masses of second class holy days, and those of Palm Sunday and the Pentecostal Vigil. This same prayer will replace the one marked ad libitum in the other masses.

5. These prayers will continue until the clergy receives notification from us that the time has come to discontinue them.

The present pastoral letter will be announced in the sermon of all parish masses (except article 4), and read during the chapter in religious communities, the first Sunday or holy day of obligation after it has been received.

H. Tétu and C.-O. Gagnon (eds.), *Mandements, lettres pastorales et circulaires des évêques de Québec* (Quebec: A Côte et Cie., 1888), Vol. 3, pp. 369-373.

DECLARATION OF THE PROVISIONAL GOVERNMENT OF LOWER CANADA, 1838

The Patriote leader, Robert Nelson, was born in Montreal in 1794. By 1834 he had become a supporter of Papineau, but he did not take part in the Rebellion of 1837. He was arrested and later released, however, and went to the United States. At a meeting in Vermont in 1838 of those who had left Canada, Nelson was elected general of an army and president of the future Canadian republic. Nelson led three to four hundred Patriotes in an invasion of Canada in February 1838. Copies of this declaration of independence were distributed in late February 1838. The Patriotes were attacked and pushed back into the United States. A second invasion in November 1838 also failed.

Whereas the solemn pact made between the people of Upper and Lower Canada, registered in the book of statutes of the United Kingdom of Great Britain and Ireland, the 31st chapter of the Acts passed in the 31st year of the Reign of George the Third (Constitutional Act of 1791) has been continually violated by the British government.

Whereas the same government has trampled under foot and usurped our rights; has disregarded and ignored our addresses, requests, protests, and remonstrations against its unconstitutional and unjust intervention in our affairs; has made use of our revenues without the constitutional consent of the local Legislature; has plundered our colonial treasury, has ordered the arrest of several of our fellow-citizens; has had them put in chains; has cast armies of mercenaries into the midst of our fields who have sown the seed of alarm, fright and consternation; whereas the same soldiery has reddened our soil with the blood of a considerable number of our compatriots, has burned our villages, has desecrated our churches, has established a most atrocious reign of terror throughout the whole country.

And whereas we can no longer tolerate these reiterated violations of our most sacred rights and patiently bear the outrages and multiplied and recent cruelties of the government of Lower Canada,

We, in the name of the people of Lower Canada, following the decrees of Divine Providence, which permits us to overthrow a government which has ignored the object and intention for which it was created and to choose the form of government best suited to establish justice, to assure domestic peace, to provide for common defence, to promote general and religious well-being and to guarantee the benefits of civil Liberty for us and for our posterity, [do solemnly declare]

1. That from this day forward the People of Lower Canada are absolved of all allegiance to Great Britain, and that all political connection between this power and Lower Canada ceases from this day onward.

2. That Lower Canada is to take the form of a Republic and now declares itself, indeed, a Republic.

3. That under the independent government of Lower Canada all citizens will have the same rights; the Indians will cease to be subject to any civil disqualification whatever, and will enjoy the same rights as the other citizens of the State of Lower Canada.

4. That any union between Church and State is declared abolished, and that any person has the right to practise freely the religion and belief his conscience dictates.

5. That Feudal or Seigneurial Tenure, is, in fact, abolished as if it had never existed in this country.

6. That any person who bears arms or supplies means of existence to the Canadian people in their fight for emancipation is relieved of all real or supposed debts or obligations towards the Seigneurs for arrears by virtue of the Seigneurial Rights existing previously.

7. That Common Jointure is entirely abolished and prohibited.

8. That imprisonment for debt will no longer exist except in cases of obvious fraud which will be specified to this effect in an act of the Legislature of Lower Canada.

9. That the death penalty will be pronounced only in cases of murder alone and in no other cases.

10. That any mortgage on real property must be the exception, and, to be valid, must be registered in the offices created for this purpose by an act of the Legislature of Lower Canada.

11. That there will be full and entire freedom of the Press in all public matters and affairs.

12. That trial by jury is guaranteed to the People of the State in its most liberal scope in criminal trials, and in civil affairs the amount of a certain sum to be determined by the Legislature of Lower Canada.

13. That as a necessity and duty of the government towards the People, public and general education will be established and particularly encouraged, as soon as circumstances permit.

14. That in order to assure franchise and freedom of election, all elections will be by means of ballot.

15. That as soon as circumstances permit, the People shall choose delegates according to the present division of the country into cities, boroughs and counties, which will constitute a Convention or Legislative Body in order to found and establish a Constitution in accordance with the needs of the country and with the resolutions of this Declaration, subject to modification according to the will of the People.

16. That any male person 21 years or over will have the right to vote, such as is provided for above, for the election of the above-named delegates.

17. That all land called "Crown" land as well as those which are called Clergy Reserves and those which are nominally in the possession of a certain company of speculators in England named "The Land Company of British North America" shall become, without need of sanction, the property of the State of Canada, with the exception of such portions of the said lands as may be in the possession of farmers who hold them in reality, for whom we guarantee titles, by virtue of a law which will be passed in order to legalize possession of such portions of land situated in the Townships, which are now under cultivation.

18. That the French and English languages shall be used in all public matters.

And for the support of this Declaration and the success of the patriotic cause we support, We, confident in the protection of the Almighty and the justice of our line of conduct, do by these resolutions, pledge solemnly and mutually, one to the other, our lives, our fortunes, and our most sacred honour.

By order of the provisional government,

Robert Nelson, President.

ARRESTS IN 1837

Occupation

farmers	244
craftsmen	56
merchants, 3 of whom were also members of the Assembly	51
commercial travellers, journeymen	41
Members of the Assembly	13
doctors, 1 of whom was also a member of the Assembly	13
innkeepers	11
notaries, 4 of whom were also members of the Assembly	10
students in law and medicine	8
journalists and printers	7
bailiffs	5
lawyers, 2 of whom were also members of the Assembly	4
teachers	2
townsmen (bourgeoisie)	2
priest	1
land surveyor	1
others	35
Total imprisoned in Montreal	**495**

Age

Under 20 years	49
20-30 years	128
30-40 years	116
40-50 years	110
50-60 years	50
Over 60 years	15
Age unknown	27
Total imprisoned in Montreal	**495**

ARRESTS IN 1838

The arrests in 1838 were more numerous than in 1837. On 4 November 1838, Sir John Colborne, the Governor of Lower Canada, declared martial law. More than 800 people were imprisoned in Montreal. Most of them were released after a few days or a few weeks in prison. On 27 November, 108 people were brought before an English military court. Nine prisoners were acquitted. Ninety-nine were sentenced to death, but this sentence was commuted for most of the prisoners. Ultimately, twenty-seven were freed on bail, two were banished, and fifty-eight were ordered deported to Australia. Twelve of those sentenced to death were executed in Montreal as follows:

December 21, 1838
J.-N. Cardinal
Joseph Duquette

January 18, 1839
P.-T. Decoigne (notary)
F.-X. Hamelin (farmer)

Joseph Robert (farmer)

A. Sanguinet (farmer, 38 years)

C. Sanguinet (farmer, 36 years, brother to the above, executed February 15, 1839)

February 15, 1839

Chevalier de Lorimier (notary, 34 years)

Amable Daunais (farmer)

Charles Hindenlang (French soldier)

P.-R. Narbonne

François Nicolas (teacher)

Note

Several of those arrested in 1837 were released after a few days or weeks in prison. By 1 June 1838, 145 were still in prison. In addition, many of those who had participated in the rebellion had left for the United States. The prisoners deported to Australia were pardoned in 1844. Those who fled to the United States received individual pardons from 1843 on. Papineau returned to Canada in 1845, and a general Amnesty Act was passed in 1849.

Chronology

LOWER CANADA, 1791-1839

1791 – Constitutional Act or Canada Act.

1822 – Union Bill introduced into the British House of Commons.
– Papineau, Cuvillier, and John Neilson go to London to secure the defeat of the Union Bill. Bill does not pass.

1828 – Report of the Canada Committee.

1829-
1832 – Period in Lower Canada when moderates and future radicals work together for reform. Some measures pass but most are defeated by the Legislative Council. Papineau and his followers still have faith that reforms can be achieved in Canada through the British constitution.

1831 – British government transfers control of most of the revenue to the Legislative Assembly, but the Assembly still refuses to grant a permanent Civil List and demands control over all revenue.

1832 – Outbreak of cholera in Lower Canada and Upper Canada brings death to many. Outbreaks occur again as emigration from Britain, especially Ireland, increases.
– In a by-election in the West Ward of Montreal, three French Canadians are killed by British troops. The event comes to be known as the Montreal Massacre.

1833 – Beginning in January, much time is spent by the Legislative Assembly investigating the Montreal Massacre.
– The Assembly obstructs the legislative program of the government, demanding an elected Legislative Council modelled after the American Senate.
– In the spring, the Assembly refuses to pass the bill for supplies.
– In June, the radicals begin urging that political unions or groups be formed throughout Lower Canada. A campaign of activism and agitation for reform is launched, patterned after the campaign in Ireland led by Daniel O'Connell.
– An outbreak of cholera among newly arrived British immigrants.

1834 – Ninety-two Resolutions pass in the Legislative Assembly.
– The Central and Permanent Committee of the District of Montreal is formed, with Edmund O'Callaghan as secretary.

– Legislative Assembly refuses to vote supplies for the second year.

– Charter granted to the British American Land Company for British settlement in the Eastern Townships.

– Radicals attack the salaries of government officials.

– Boycott is organized against imported goods in order to reduce the amount of customs revenue available to the government.

– In the November elections the radicals win a sweeping victory.

1835   – Those supporting the government begin to form Constitutional Associations.

– The radicals urge the formation of Reform Associations.

– Lord Gosford arrives in August as Governor of Lower Canada. He is also to head a commission which will advise the British government on a course of action for Lower Canada.

1836   – Crop failure in Lower Canada.

1837   – Major economic depression occurs in British North America, Britain, and the United States.

– Radicals continue the boycott and urge that goods be smuggled from the United States.

– Petitions urging reforms are sent to Britain.

– In March, the Gosford Commission reports that there is no progress and that there will be no concessions.

– Four days after the report by the Gosford Commission, word arrives of Lord John Russell's Resolutions.

– During April and May, the Quebec City *Patriotes* under Etienne Parent's leadership attack the Montreal *Patriotes* for their political methods. The English press becomes particularly virulent in its attacks on the *Patriotes*.

– On July 4, the *Patriote* newspapers print the American Declaration of Independence and apply its ideas to the situation in Lower Canada.

– On August 29, a motion introduced in the Legislative Assembly declaring it to be the duty of the House to maintain its fidelity to the Crown and to cement the connection of Lower Canada with Britain is defeated by a vote of 63 to 16.

– On October 4, the Sons of Liberty issue an appeal.

– Soldiers are sent to Deux-Montagnes by Gosford because of the disaffection rapidly growing in the county.

– On October 24, Bishop Lartigue issues a *mandement* warning against rebellion.

– On October 31, Tory supporters in Montreal clash with *Patriote* supporters. The *Patriotes* are routed and the offices of the *Vindicator* are wrecked.

– Papineau, O'Callaghan, Wolfred Nelson, Thomas Storrow Brown, and others flee to the Richelieu Valley.

– Warrants are issued for the arrest of the *Patriote* leaders.

– On November 23, a clash between government troops and *Patriote* supporters occurs at St.-Denis. Papineau and others escape to the United States.

– On November 25, resistance at St. Charles is broke.

– In December, soldiers and English militia defeat the *Patriotes* at St. Eustache.

1838   – Second uprising and an invasion of Lower Canada from the United States occurs in November. The *Patriotes* led by Robert Nelson are defeated.

1839   – Lord Durham's *Report* is made public.

PROJECT TEAM

Patrick Douglas – Head of History at Monarch Park Secondary School, Toronto Board of Education.

A. F. Flow – Social Studies Consultant with the Toronto Board of Education and former Head of History at Lawrence Park Collegiate, Toronto Board of Education.

Alex Hewlitt – Vice-Principal at Tabor Park Vocational School, former Chairman of Social and Environmental Sciences at L'Amoreaux Collegiate, and former Head of History at Cedarbrae Collegiate, Scarborough Board of Education.

Robert M. Laxer – Professor at the Ontario Institute for Studies in Education.

Stan Pearl – Chairman of Social and Environmental Sciences at L'Amoreaux Collegiate, former Head of History at Woburn Collegiate, and former teacher at Cedarbrac Collegiate, Scarborough Board of Education.

Virginia R. Robeson – Project Co-ordinator of the Montreal/Toronto Research Group and Research Officer at the Ontario Institute for Studies in Education.

Eric R. Skeoch – Head of History at Malvern Collegiate, and former teacher at Lawrence Park Collegiate, Toronto Board of Education.

Peter D. Stille – Head of Guidance at Bickford Park High School, and former teacher of history at Oakwood Collegiate, Toronto Board of Education.

K. C. Tancock – Head of History at Sir Wilfrid Laurier Collegiate, Scarborough Board of Education.

IN COLLABORATION WITH

Michel Allard – Professor at the Université du Québec à Montréal.

Yolande Capistran-Phaneuf – Teacher with the Commission des Ecoles catholiques de Montréal.

Aurore Dupuis – Teacher with the Commission des Ecoles catholiques de Montréal.

André Francoeur – Teacher with the Commission des Ecoles catholiques de Montréal.

Paul-M. Moussette – Teacher with the Commission scolaire régionale Honoré-Mercier.

Robert Savoie – Teacher with the Commission des Ecoles catholiques de Montréal.

ACKNOWLEDGMENTS

We gratefully acknowledge the following sources for permission to use their materials.
J. Ross Robertson Collection, Metropolitan Toronto Central Library, for the photographs.

Holt, Rinehart and Winston of Canada Limited, for the excerpt in Document 44.

24